THE BUGS DOCTOR

with a Passion for music

MY AUTOBIOGRAPHY

by

Emmanuel M Ndawula

Grosvenor House
Publishing Limited

First Published in Great Britain in 2015 by Emmanuel M. Ndawula.

The right of Emmanuel Ndawula to be identified as the author of this
work has been asserted by him in accordance with Section 78
of the Copyright, Designs and Patents Act 1988

The book cover picture is copyright to Emmanuel Ndawula

This book is published by
Grosvenor House Publishing Ltd
28-30 High Street, Guildford, Surrey, GU1 3EL.
www.grosvenorhousepublishing.co.uk

A CIP record for this book
is available from the British Library

ISBN 978-1-78148-367-1

I have written this book in memory of my parents who sacrificed a lot for my education. I dedicate it to all their descendants, to my wife Lillian and all health care professionals all over the world.

Contents

Acknowledgements

I would like to thank close members of my family who helped me on this long journey. Over the years, they put up with my frequent absence from home as well as long hours of work at my desk at home.

I thank my wife Lillian who patiently read through the manuscript looking for glaring errors as well as listening to me reading extracts from the manuscript to find out if they made sense to a non-medical person. I also thank my two sons, Bobby and Paulo who had a quick read through the last version of the manuscript and made some constructive comments.

Last but not least, I thank all the health care staff I worked with over the years. I was lucky to work with some of the most dedicated professionals anybody could wish to be teammates with.

Preface

This is a narrative of my life as a young person born in Uganda, as a microbiologist and a singer-song writer. There are many stories and sub stories in this long journey from rural Africa to leafy Kent, England. I have written the story in such a way that I share my memories with the various people – schoolmates, relatives, workmates and many others who may have had similar experiences. Then to you the reader, a person maybe I have never met, I say, 'Please enjoy the ride'.

I go through my early life, relationship with my parents and the excellent education I had at one of the best boarding schools in Uganda. The transition from school to University was quite fascinating. The experience at medical school and as an intern demonstrated how the necessary skills to be a doctor were acquired. I mention my mentor and discuss the topic of role models.

To the people who do not know what a medical microbiologist does, I reveal my-day to-day activities, which I will show are relevant to everybody who has had an infection or will have an infection and that means everybody. Information is also given to young people who may want to pursue a career in clinical microbiology.

I introduce a concept of descriptive diagnosis, which I used when formulating antimicrobial guidelines. Hopefully, this will help doctors to 'fine tune' the way they diagnose and treat infections. It also enables patients to understand management of their infections.

I give an account of my other role – the Infection Control Doctor (ICD) and the qualities I believe people should look for in a Director of Infection Prevention and Control (DIPC), the supremo of infection control in every Trust in the UK. I give brief demystifying descriptions of MRSA and Clostridium difficile – two notorious pathogens, which have been splashed as headlines in the popular press.

There are examples of anonymised cases of specific infections. People who have suffered such infections, doctors and nurses who looked after them will remember the experiences. The roles of clinicians and microbiologists are clearly defined. Let us compare notes.

For quite a long time, I had a wonderful bureaucratic- free working relationship with General Practitioners who sent a large number of specimens to our laboratories.

The climax is the NHS, which has the longest chapter. I use the descriptive diagnosis concept to tell you the root causes of the problems in the NHS. I suggest remedies and cite the proposals that I sent to our politicians of both main parties when they invited ideas. The remedies save money and improve the quality of care. Although this applies to the UK health service, there are many principles that are universal.

The other activities that may be of interest to many people are meetings and interviews. I invite you to share some funny and serious experiences.

Has anybody in your organisation urged you to embrace change or else? I share my experiences with you.

As a person who has worked in both public and private healthcare systems, I compare and contrast some aspects of the two systems.

On a lighter note, I tell a narrative of my passion for creative music and share my views on a variety of topics through the medium of music.

Last but not least, I have had moments of reflection, which I think have made me a better person. I share these with you.

Enjoy the book.

1

My Early Years

My journey starts in Fort Portal hospital where I was born in 1947. This was the largest hospital in the Kingdom of Toro, western Uganda nearest to Humura parish, Kyaka County, where my father was posted as the Native Anglican Church (NAC) priest in 1946. My father Ananiya Kasigala was born in 1906 in a village of Nabubaale, Buyamba sub-county in another small Kingdom of Kooki (now part of Buganda Kingdom) about 100 miles south east of Fort Portal. He was the son of Mwegereko, son of Busweswe, son of Nyamulumba, who was son of King Bwowe. That is the formal traditional way of introducing a muganda as lineage is passed down along patrilineal lines.

The next level of identification is the 'clan' system. A clan is a group of people who can trace their lineage to a common ancestor. Each of the fifty-two clans in Buganda (the largest kingdom in Uganda) is symbolised by a totem (an animal or plant) and royal name by which it is known by or group of royals with common ancestry. We belong to the Babiito (royal name) clan. I am a Mubiito (a person of the Babiito clan) as the children tradition-ally belong to the father's clan. My mother Eseza Kasigala was the daughter of Sedulaka Mbugelamula of the Ngabi (Bushbuck) clan. Mother, like her father, belonged to the Ngabi clan. Her mother Eseri Namaganda Lwamala was of Nte (Cow) clan. My grand-mother Eseri spent a lot of time in Kampala (the capital of Uganda) as a lady in waiting for the Namasole (mother of the then King of Buganda – Sir Frederick Mutesa II).

At baptism when I was one week old; two names were given to me – Emmanuel as the Christian name and Mwesigwa, which means 'honest' as the surname. Some born again Christians, as my parents were, did not give their children clan names. Instead, they used names of virtue like 'kindness', charity', 'hope' among others. I added 'Ndawula' as the clan and surname when I became of age and Mwesigwa became my middle name. I picked the name from a list of names I got from my cousin, the late Deborah Kiwanuka. Her father, Nasanairi Mulira took in my father and looked after him because my grandfather died before my father was born. The name 'Kasigala' denotes, 'the little one stayed' in the womb.

I get flashes of memories of when I was very young. I remember a rainy day and loud thunder and my father coming home in the evening and reporting that a little girl had been killed by lightning. He said that she had been thrown across the classroom. He went on to advise us that it was not a good idea to shout when it was raining and for a long time I held that view that shouting during a rainstorm was dangerous. There were many such 'never dos' which were associated with 'dangerous' consequences. Some were for our benefit as children while others were for the convenience of the parents.

The other flashback was walking from home with my mother, across a stream to a rock on which she ground millet, which was the staple food in that part of the country at the time. This illustrates the important role women played and still play in the provision of food for their families. Later on when I reminded my parents of these events, they told me that I was around four years when they happened.

In 1952 we were posted to Iganga in Busoga Kingdom, which is in the eastern part of Uganda. The following year, I started school. It was a preparatory school, which was a stone's throw from our house – a two-minute walk by a short – cut through a bushy hedge separating our garden and the school. On the first day of school my father walked with me to school taking the long route of about half a mile. My parents later told me that they had been impressed by the fact that I never used the short cut. This could be the first glimpse of my character of obedience and non-adventurism.

One evening in 1953, my father arrived home on his bike at quite a speed, dismounted and walked quickly to where we were sitting in the courtyard and said 'The Kabaka has been exiled'. He was reporting the banishment of Sir Edward Frederick Mutesa, the Kabaka (the King of Buganda) to Britain. My father hardly talked about politics. His main topic of discussion was religion and faith. The fact that he reported this event to the rest of the family indicates how close the Baganda (people of the Buganda Kingdom) were and still are to their King.

At the beginning of 1954, we moved again. This time westwards to a place called Makonzi in Mubende District. I started my primary education that year. My first teacher was called Solome Nabukenya who, as I remember, usually wore a nice green hat. I mention this because she wore it almost all of the time and it became a subject of gossip among my schoolmates. She was a wonderful teacher who taught us the times tables, reading and writing as well as many folk songs, which I thoroughly enjoyed. She and my mother were friends. Another interesting little fact is that she was of the same clan as my mother – the Ngabi clan and this cemented their friendship.

One of the main events of 1955 was the return of Sir Edward Mutesa from exile. Months before he returned, I remember seeing many lorries carrying jubilant volunteers on their way to Kampala to do up the palace. On his return, as expected, there were celebrations everywhere. When he visited our nearest town Kasanda, our whole family went to join the cheering crowds. It was an exciting time.

Most people have a particular teacher who plays a pivotal role in their education. This happened to me in 1958 when a teacher called Sajjabi joined our school. He was a short hairy man with a receding hairline but a very good teacher. Up to that time, all the subjects were taught in our local language, Luganda. Aged eleven, I knew very few words of English. By the end of that year, this wonderful teacher had taught me enough English to be able to stage a short play in which I played the main character – a librarian. This was very special to me because the play was at the end of year speech day in the presence of my parents who were the guests of honour.

3

In 1959, I passed the primary leaving examination and moved to Kako Junior School about 100 miles away. It was a day school and therefore I stayed with relatives on my maternal side. The return journey to school was about 10 miles on foot. Life was full of challenges marked by very poor diet consisting of mainly cassava (which sometimes was bitter) and beans. While there, I missed my favourite dish of mashed matooke (plantain) and meat or fish stew. There was also a lot of hard manual labour.

It was a hot Saturday afternoon but I was quite comfortable in the shade of a large tree in the forest from where I collected firewood. I tied the last knot firmly making sure that the firewood bundle was quite secure and that the small twigs would not fall out; then I put a cushion (called 'enkata' in Luganda) made out of banana leaves to protect my head from the sharp bits of the firewood. I was in a crouching position about to lift the bundle when I instinctively glanced behind me. I froze. There was this huge snake just a few feet from my heels. I could see its black eyes and its forked tongue flicking in and out of its tight mouth. It glided past me into neighbouring undergrowth. I looked around in case there was another creature nearby. There was none. With trembling arms, I quickly put the bundle on my sweating head and hurried along a narrow path leading out of the forest to the bright sunshine at the bottom of the hill. As I ascended, I kept on saying to myself, 'One step back –oh no it is too horrible to think about'. It was a narrow escape. This was a one off scary encounter with a snake. Later on, when I told friends and relatives of the incident, they all said that it was a rare event to see snakes in the countryside contrary to what city dwellers thought.

While still at this residence, one event endeared me to my parents. It was one hot Saturday afternoon; my sweaty head was half buried in the bundle of firewood I was carrying. As I came to the top of the hill with the dark forest well behind me, I tilted my head slightly to see the red tiled house I lived in. The door was wide open. This was unusual as it was always closed. I threw the firewood on the ground and walked towards the door. I could hear voices – they sounded like my parents. As I walked through the door and my eyes adjusting from the bright sunshine outside to relative darkness inside, now I could see – they were my parents. With that worried look on her face, my mother said, 'Eh – my child, you look tired – you have lost weight'.

As I was greeting them, Mrs Kisule, the owner of the house came through the door and said, 'Oh you are back from the forest –welcome back'.

'Thanks madam,' I replied glancing at my mother who still had that worried look on her face. She had come to collect a teapot and tea cosy. She went back to the kitchen, which was part of another house across the courtyard, giving me a chance to talk to my parents. Father leaned forward and whispered 'Are you alright son?'

'Fine dad, really fine,' I replied in an assuring manner.

After tea, it was time to bid them farewell. They had brought some nice things for me – bread and juice. As they left my father said, 'There, buy some more bread with this; make sure you don't go hungry' as he handed 20 shillings to me. This was equivalent to £1 at the time.

During the following holidays, my father suggested looking for alternative accommodation, but I reassured him that as it was the last year before going to another school, I would persevere.

On the eve of going back to school, after giving me the school fees, my father said, 'Here is the pocket money,' putting forty shillings in my hand.

I said, 'No dad, I do not need all that much, I still have some 10 shillings left from the 20 you gave me when you visited me'.

He insisted, 'Take it; we do not want you to go hungry as you study for your exams'.

This and the fact I saved them the trouble of looking for alternative accommodation endeared me to my parents forever. Years later, when I told them that I did not have money they knew I was telling them the truth. Trust had been established. At that time little did I know that I would many years later write a song on the subject of trust. The title is 'Have I Done Enough To Be Trusted?'

The teachers at the junior school were very supportive, in particular Stanley Kizza who was the deputy headmaster. He and my father were friends and born again Christians. I am still in touch with one of his sons, Malcolm Kizza who now resides in the UK.

At the end of 1961, I passed my Senior Entrance Examination and got a place at the school of my first choice – King's College Budo. Three students from Kako were admitted to Budo. I was one of them. The other two were Harriet Namutebi and Edward Kakooza. The admission system to all good schools was based purely on merit.

2

Life at King's College Budo

When I arrived at the school for the first time I was awestruck by the size of the place; the huge library arch had a yellowish plaque (with the year 1906) against the red bricks, which most old buildings were built of. As I looked at the mixture of ancient and modern buildings consisting of dormitories, classrooms, houses for teachers not to mention an old chapel, which had been converted to a library, I imagined generations of important people in the distant and recent past who had occupied them. At that moment I realised that I was at the beginning of a life changing experience.

King's College Budo is a special school to me and many Ugandans, as well as the many teachers who taught there. It boasts among its Alumni, kings, presidents, ministers and many more who have contributed to the development of Uganda as well as organisations outside Uganda. Initially established to educate the sons of 'chiefs', it soon started admitting Ugandans from all walks of life based purely on merit. I remember occasions one of the pupils related to the King of Buganda being brought to the school in a Rolls Royce while others came by taxi.

Like many schools in Uganda, it was founded by missionaries. Children of the clergy, even at the time I joined the school, paid reduced school fees. Its students were among the first to sit the Cambridge School Certificate examination in 1936. It was the first to admit girls in 1933, making it the first coeducational school of higher learning in Uganda. In 1935, it produced the first group of girls to pass the highly competitive examinations into Makerere College.

The dormitories or houses as we preferred to call them were named after the countries of the commonwealth and some prominent people. They included Australia, Canada, England, Ghana, Mutesa, Nigeria (added later) South Africa (later renamed Africa), Gaster, Grace and Sabaganzi. The last three were girls' dormitories. My dormitory was Ghana House.

Life does not happen in blocks as other unexpected things do occur and have to be dealt with simultaneously. In November 1963, my beloved grandmother, Eseri Lwamala passed away after an abdominal operation for an intestinal obstruction. The last time I had seen her was in 1959, when my sister Deborah and I had visited her home in a small village called Kiswaga in Kooki County. She had told us many stories of her life as the lady in waiting for Namasole (our Queen Mother at the time). She was being looked after by my uncle, Isakari Buye (my mother's step-brother). It was a very sad event for the whole family but life had to continue.

Back to my new school – the majority of the teachers were expatriates from the UK. The headmaster at the time was Ian Robinson, a tall man with a powerful presence whenever he walked into the school assembly. He had an interesting mannerism of holding his papers (if they were few) with his right hand stretched behind his back. As expected from this composition of teachers, there was a lot of cricket and Shakespeare. In fact the school staged many of the Shakespearean plays, at least one every year. English lessons were taught by the popular Mr Wareham, a very nice man who walked with a slight limp, never asked any questions during class, thus his popularity. Instead, he read to the class Bulldog Drummond books, which were a real treat for us. He would make natural pauses as he glanced obliquely at the ceiling. Everybody looked forward to his next English lesson and we all learnt a lot about pronunciation, intonation, ambience among others, which he emphasised as important skills in communication.

There was a Ugandan teacher who also taught us English. His name was Olopot. I remember studying the book, *Cry the Beloved Country* with him. For the first time I become aware of what was going on in South Africa. In fact around that time the dormitory which was called South Africa was renamed Africa.

The other Ugandan teachers included Enoch Mulira (who was my cousin) – he taught English and religious studies, Sempebwa who was deputy headmaster, Ssali who taught Luganda and Kisaka who taught art. We had two American teachers – Buchanan and Taylor. The latter was a mathematics teacher who really increased my interest in that subject. Taylor was also the housemaster of Ghana house for a while.

Every Saturday morning, there was an inspection of the dormitories. This involved early morning cleaning of the dormitory, making our beds properly and standing by our clean lockers as the housemaster inspected each student's area, one at a time. One memorable Saturday morning, Taylor came in and announced, 'Boys, there will be no inspection today. President Kennedy has been assassinated'.

There was total silence – you could hear a pin drop. This was Saturday 23 November 1963. The tragic event had happened the day before on 22 November.

The American teachers introduced basketball to the school. I was a member of the school team, which had privileges including special diets and trips to other schools for matches. That is what young people these days would call 'cool'. Talking about diet, there was one man whom everybody in the school knew and respected. He was called Kangave, an unassuming short man who walked with short little steps, stooping forward. He was in charge of the school kitchen. As teenagers, food was very important to us and we always looked forward to meal times.

Discipline was a very important pillar of school life. One early evening when we were in the middle of the sports field, I overhead orchestrated conversation between a sports master and a pupil.

'Who cares?' the boy said shrugging his shoulders.

'You care, fifty reds,' the teacher responded sternly.

'Who cares?' the boy continued as the other boys gathered around.

'You care, one hundred reds,' the teacher shouted pointing at him.

Unbelievably the boy continued softly, 'I really don't care'.

The teacher was by now seething with rage as he finally said, 'Two hundred reds and you are in the book!'

'Who cares?' was quite a common saying in pupil-to-pupil conversations, but for goodness sake, not with a teacher. The boy had a moment of insanity. Within a matter of minutes the teacher had gone through all the common levels of punishment for misconduct. 'Reds' was a piece of paper with red lines. The punishment of fifty reds was to fill in that paper with fifty words from a textbook. Being put in the book meant carrying a basin full of stones on a Saturday afternoon from a nearby quarry to another site about two hundred yards away. The other misconducts included walking on grass, walking about during the rest period when everybody was meant to be lying on their beds. Many old Budonians I talked to years later said that the discipline did us a lot of good. It also engrained in us the notion that actions have consequences.

We had some fun as well. We always looked forward to Easter time when we sang Easter hymns and decorated our dormitories. It was the only day we visited all dormitories including girls' dormitories to look at the decorations. It was really exciting.

I also remember Saturday entertainment, which included some very good films and concerts, not to mention end of term house parties at which songs by the Beatles, Cliff Richard and Elvis were very popular.

There was also a memorable weekly event that happened every Sunday evening. Most pupils would put on their Sunday best and go for a walk. When I had time, I would take a long walk, which involved going through the sports fields past the girls' dormitory to the furthest boundaries of the school then back in time for the weekly roll call. For the short walk, I visited the school zoo, which had a number of attractions including ostriches, antelopes and other smaller grass-eating animals.

In 1965 our group in senior four was called the 'Spearheads'. That was the level at which we were allowed to have the maiden dancing evening with girls of the same class at Gayaza High School, a boarding girls only school which was about twenty miles from our school. We had been waiting for this for years as we had heard many exciting stories told by generation of boys ahead of our class. The venues alternated. It was our turn to go to their school.

We were filled with anxiety and excitement as we boarded the school bus which on this occasion was driven by none other than the headmaster Mr Robinson himself. A few miles before we arrived, the bus stopped. He stood up to face us. 'Get out the bus and freshen up. Look sharp boys,' he said with a wry smile. We all got out, stretched our legs, straightened our ties and got back on the bus again.

We arrived at the school, got out the bus and stood together in a group. As we gazed at the buildings around us, we could see many heads in the windows peeping at us. Later on, I was told that these were girls of the lower classes waiting for their turn in years to come.

Soon our hostesses came and joined us. There were some boys who had friends and acquaintances that came and took them away on a tour. Those who did not know anybody gathered in small groups. I was talking to friends in our group, when I heard a soft voice behind me say 'Hello'. I turned round to face this very nice girl very close to me.

'May I take you around?' she continued. Needless, to say the rest of the evening went very well. She became my girlfriend for the next six years. Most of this time, she was studying in the UK. Geographical separation can affect relationships but that is another story.

Years passed quickly and before long, I did my O Levels and went back for my A levels to do Physics, Chemistry and Biology. My favourite subject was Physics because once I learnt the laws, I could easily solve problems. Among many pupils, there was a mind-set of hard work, competition and yearning to do well. Posting the end of term examination results on notice boards for all to see drove most people into a frenzy of intense competition. One may argue that it was good preparation for adult life outside.

Many people including myself woke up in the middle of the night to study. This 'illegal' activity was colloquially called 'eating fire'.

I completed my education at Budo and got a place in the Makerere University Medical School. This was in 1968. Why did I go into Medicine? The decision was very easy. It was really a group decision. The majority of science students who did Physics, Chemistry and Biology went to medical school and those who did double Mathematics and Physics went into engineering. There were not many other choices. That year, the group that went to medical school included Arthur Bikangaga (went to USA), Dafala, John Iga, Albert Kaddumukasa, Sam Lutalo, Godfrey Luyombya, James Olobo-Lalobo, Joel Okulo, James Mugisha, Semambo and Florence Mirembe who was the only girl in the group. She went on to become Professor and head of Obstetrics and Gynaecology at Mulago Hospital where we trained. We all remembered the school moto 'Gakyali Mabaga' in Luganda (the language of Baganda) translated as 'so little done, so much to do'. Armed with this and what we believed was a good education, we were ready to face the world outside the protected environment of a boarding school.

3

My Eyes are Opened

It was the last day at school. I had been waiting for her to collect me since nine o'clock. It was now eleven. To pass time, I decided to go to the library for the last time. I told a housemate who was to be collected in late afternoon where I was going. I sat in the library and started flipping through pages of the books that lay on the table – the sort of thing you do in doctor's waiting room. I had just settled on one page when at the corner of my left eye, I saw a group of people coming my way. I turned. It was the housemate leading the way. He pointed in my direction as I stood up to meet them. A very nice lady was leading the way.

'Mwesigwa?' she inquired.

'Yes', I responded with as wide a smile as my mouth could manage.

'I am Robinah and this is Steven', she said pointing to a man standing by her side. 'We've come to collect you'. Off we went to my dormitory to collect my stuff and headed for Kampala.

Going slightly back to March 1967 when my sister Deborah went to Britain for further studies in nursing, she had requested this close friend of hers Robinah Kabugo to help me look for a job in my long vacation before university. This kind lady with her friend Steven Magambo looked after me very well.

They got a job for me in a book firm called Uganda School Supplies. After a few weeks, I got a better job in the department of statistics – Ministry of Economic Development at Entebbe. I stayed with Steven at Nakulabye – a small town in the suburbs of Kampala. I commuted by communal taxis to and from Entebbe (twenty miles away) daily. At the place of work, my job was filing cards of a variety of data collected from the whole country. I also copied documents using a gestetner duplicator machine, which I found very interesting to use once I got the hang of manually setting it up and turning its big drum to start producing copies.

I worked with some interesting and funny people. One of these was a man called Mwangi, a Kenyan. He described all the people we knew by sign language. He would say, 'This morning, there was a very heavy police escort to the airport accompanying...' He would then pat the top of his head with his hands. He was referring to President Obote who styled his hair the way Mwangi was demonstrating. He would portray many people known to us including female members of staff by demonstrating noticeable parts of their bodies. He was really funny. It was hilarious.

Back to Nakulabye, for the first time, I went to a nightclub and drank half a glass of beer. All those around our table, laughed at me teasingly for ordering such a small amount of drink. Then Steven came to my rescue saying, 'Leave the boy alone, he has just left school'. This was followed by a louder bout of laughter almost drowning the then very popular Congolese music from the nearby loudspeaker. Some of the people around me at the time were smokers, but I never started the habit. I always remembered what my father used to say about smoking, 'it is like burning notes of money'. From an early age I had learnt to do all other things in moderation.

Nakulabye was a lively town especially on weekends. It had many bars and nightclubs. Every night there were these thunderous poundings of music; making it difficult to sleep but I soon got used to it. The adaptability of the human ear is amazing. I spent a lot of time reading novels and listening to music on radio.

I learned to live within my small budget but most of all I learnt how to manage my time – which was to be an invaluable skill for the future. In these few months, my eyes were opened to the world outside a boarding school. I had lived quite a sheltered life, which I must say I loved but it was time to move into adult life. By the time I went to University, I had been acclimatised to the life outside a boarding school.

4

Medical School

I was sitting in the middle of a class of more than a hundred, wondering what the first day would bring, when the side door to the lecture theatre swung open and in walked this short elderly man with silver hair. He came to an abrupt stop and stood looking above our heads with his arms straight down his sides. He said in clear voice, 'I am standing in anatomical position with palms facing you...' This was the beginning of the first lecture in medical school by Professor Haines, head of Anatomy. By the end the week, those who could not stand the sight of dissecting dead bodies dropped out. It was also the beginning of hard work and monthly tests. This first year group of medical students consisted of more than a hundred people who came from the whole of East Africa (Kenya, Uganda and Tanzania) as at that time, Makerere was the University of East Africa. With pooled resources from the three countries, there was a high calibre collection of tutors, lecturers and professors.

The other good teacher in anatomy was Professor Sebuwufu who helped us to remember facts by giving wonderful analogies, some with sexual innuendoes. There was another anatomy lecturer who I thought was a chain smoker. One day, I struck a conversation with him as we worked on the anatomy of the upper arm. I asked, 'Sir, Why do you smoke so much when you know that smoking is not good for you?' Without a moment's hesitation he replied, 'Son, it is good to live fifty good years than a hundred miserable years craving for a cigarette'. At that early stage in my training, I learnt that in preventive medicine, knowledge or information alone is not enough to change behaviour. I always remember that when I think of people making lifestyle choices. Unfortunately, in real life these choices in most cases affect other people.

Before we could go anywhere near a patient, we had to study several other subjects including physiology (study of the way the body works), biochemistry (study of chemical processes in the body), pharmacology (study of how drugs work in the body) and microbiology (study of organisms-viruses, bacteria, fungi and parasites). Two of these subjects were noteworthy – pharmacology and microbiology for my future career.

Dr Donald McIntosh was a very good lecturer on pharmacology while Doctor and later on Professor Sultan Karim at that time carried out some very good research on a group of chemicals called prostaglandins and their effect on childbirth. Understanding of basic pharmacology would prepare me for my career as a microbiologist who must know in detail how antimicrobial drugs are handled by the body.

Professor Nochiri was the head of microbiology. He originally came from Nigeria. He came to Uganda via the UK where he returned after his work. He was a parasitologist – a person specialising in parasites –worms, malaria and other such organisms. He was renowned for issuing detailed handouts to students. Little did I know at the time that I would follow in his footsteps and become a microbiologist who must have a vast knowledge of all organisms that cause infections and drugs that treat them.

At the end the third year, just before I did clinical work, I was lucky to get a job at Kilembe Mines hospital about 200 miles south west of Kampala. I worked with two medical officers. One of them was Dr Nsamba who was my schoolmate. Our fathers were friends. He gave me a crash programme of learning how to deal with common conditions in outpatients. The other person who showed me the ropes was a fourth year medical student by the name of Sabuka. He was from Tanzania. Before long I was sitting on my own desk and telling the attending nurse, 'Next patient please'. Wait a minute. My treatments had to be checked by my seniors before they could be given to patients.

During vacations in my fourth year, I also worked at Iganga Hospital, which was one of the many 'one hundred – bed' hospitals built in rural areas at the time. They were very well – equipped with adequate staffing levels. Iganga hospital was in eastern Uganda very near my first primary school (*see chapter 1*). At this hospital, I worked with some wonderful doctors including Dr Abaru and Dr David Mukasa who were medical superintendents of the hospital at different times. They gave me one to one teaching on a wide variety of clinical conditions.

Back to medical school, there were other clinical teachers who made an impact on us in such a way that when we met again years later, we talked about them. I will mention a few. Professor German, a good communicator, was a psychiatrist who was liked by all students for his exceptional ability to impart knowledge. There was the unforgettable Professor Latima Musoke with his catchword 'remember', which he used in every other sentence. He was a very good paediatrician. There were many other good lecturers who gave us their all to make sure we became good doctors.

In the fourth and fifth years, we had some training in ENT (Ear, Nose and Throat), Ophthalmology, Public Health, Anaesthetics and Statistics. The latter normally a dull subject was made very interesting by Dr Stephen Lwanga. Little did I know at the time, that it will be a vital subject in the understanding and interpretation of data in medical literature later in my career.

One event we all cherished was the Grand Round, which was a case conference attended various experts. The lecture theatre was filled to capacity. The case was presented by the team who looked or were still looking after the patient. They revealed the information piecemeal intercepted by frantic discussions and opinions from the attending experts as we medical students and junior doctors listened attentively. The suspense was unbearable. Then the final arbiter, the pathologist took to the stage; showed his slides and announced the final diagnosis. Such events were educational and I attended many in my long career.

The social life at the university was quite hectic but balanced. I believed and still do, even more now, that birds of the same feathers flock together. My close friends were fellow medical student. We believed in hard work followed by relaxing good time. The friends included Godfrey Luyombya with whom I shared a room in Mitchell hall of residence for the first few years of Medical School. He went on to become a consultant psychiatrist working in the UK. The other friends also in Mitchell hall were Albert Kaddumukasa and Shad Mukembo who both became medical practitioners in UK.

On 16 March 1973, I graduated as a doctor. It was a beautiful sunny day. My parents attended the graduation ceremony. Needless to say, they were very happy and proud of what I had achieved.

5

The Internship

I woke up to the rumbling noise of traffic and the occasional sound of a car horn on a busy road nearby. As a schoolboy and later as an undergraduate, I had developed an accurate biological clock to wake up very early in the morning. I had also mastered the act of getting ready for action in record time. With my white coat on and stethoscope in my pocket I was soon on my way, closing the door of the Doctors' Mess behind me. This was the first day of my internship. This was the day I was going to be officially as addressed as 'Doctor Ndawula'. Indeed as I walked passed the nurses' hostel, a group of nurses smiled and said, 'Good morning doctor'.

'Good morning ladies', I replied with assured confidence as if I had done this for years. I made my way to the fifth floor of the main hospital.

Mulago hospital was a gift to Uganda from the British Government at the time of independence. This is where I did my training and internship. It was a huge complex consisting of six floors and had two functional units – the small administration block and the clinical areas. The administration block was on the fourth floor. As medical students, the many trips we made from the nearby medical school to the hospital took us through the administration block, which was divided by a long corridor. On the right was the works department, which was responsible for the provision of the 'hotel' services – food, electricity, water and many others. It was headed by a hospital administrator. On the left was the clinical administration, which was headed by a medical superintendent and chief nursing officer. The incumbent medical superintendent at the time was Dr Kyewalabye; a very friendly man who looked a bit drowsy the few times I met him in the corridor. He looked immaculate in his white coat although he hardly ever treated patients. He was the main link between the hospital and the Ministry of Health, which was about twenty miles away at Entebbe. Unlike modern medical directors, he had very little to do with the day-to-day work of most clinical staff. Likewise, the Ministry of Health hardly influenced the general running of the hospital. Decades later, I would frequently look back at this management structure as the 'good old days' because of its stability.

The other interesting thing about the clinical departments was that they were geographically separate; for example the whole of the fourth floor of the clinical block was General Medicine whereas the fifth was allocated to Obstetrics and Gynaecology. Each floor was subdivided into three sections – A, B and C, with each section headed by a senior consultant. A prominent surgeon at the time, Professor Ian McAdam (later Sir Ian McAdam) was in charge of ward 2A. His ward rounds included the inspection of toilets because he believed that the cleanliness of the toilets was a reflection of the standard of hygiene in the rest of the ward. If things were not up to scratch, he had the power to do something about it. Many years later, when I became an infection control doctor, I appreciated the value of that management structure and practice.

The internship year consisted of six months of Obstetrics and Gynaecology and six months of Paediatrics. As an intern, life was extremely busy but I was eager to put all the knowledge I had acquired as a medical student into practice. In obstetrics, I worked under two very good consultants – Mr Lwanga, a softly spoken, humble but very experienced doctor, and Mr Kirunda, a young physically and mentally smart man, who had just completed his postgraduate education in the UK. Many years later, he was to become a full time politician and a minister of internal affairs. The training and supervision we got was excellent and only matched by the challenges we had.

Friday evening would be the start of my weekend shift in the maternity ward and I would be sitting talking to the ever-helpful midwives as we waited for the next patient. Typically, they would wheel in a short unbooked prim gravida (meaning first pregnancy with no antenatal care) and unlikely to deliver normally because of her height. She would be bawling because of the painful contractions. History would reveal that she had taken herbal medicines – maybe the cause of the powerful contractions. The baby's heart rate would be slow and feeble. On top of that, the young woman would be very anaemic. Quick thinking and decisive actions were essential to save the two lives. In most such cases, there was a successful outcome. The sight of a group of women with their newly born babies waiting to be taken to the post-delivery ward was quite gratifying. This meant a lot to the whole team, which consisted of the midwives, interns, senior house officers, registrars and consultants. They had all made a contribution.

Paediatrics was equally busy. I lost count of the number of lumbar punctures (a procedure for taking fluid from the back to make or rule out a diagnosis of meningitis) I performed. The other very common presentation was dehydration (loss of body fluids) as a result of diarrhoea and vomiting. This is a life threatening condition. In severe cases, fluids had to be replaced through veins which in a small dehydrated child would be next to impossible to find. If you are lucky to find one, it was most likely to be on the shaven head. Then you had to try your best to establish a steady intravenous flow of the lifesaving fluid. That would not be the end of your endeavours. 'Doctor, the drip is not running', would be the voice of a nurse at the other end of the telephone as you had just put your head on the pillow in the duty room. You would rush back and find a swollen insertion site. Any slight movement of the drip would dislodge the needle from the vein into the surrounding tissues. Tired as you are, you have to find a new site if the baby's life is to be saved.

Despite our efforts, many babies died contributing to the high infant mortality rates, which were typical of the developing countries at the time. The infections included gastroenteritis, malaria bronchopneumonia, measles and hookworm infestation that caused severe anaemia – to mention but a few. All these were compounded by another major problem of malnutrition with clinical presentation as kwashiorkor and marasmus. When they survived and put on weight, their appearance was beyond recognition. I still remember their happy faces.

The other notable activity I participated in was the running of outpatient clinics for children with sickle cell disease. As expected, there is a high incidence of this condition in Africa. Sickle cell is an inherited blood disorder in which haemoglobin, the molecule which carries oxygen is defective. I have a trait of this condition. I am lucky not to have a double dose of the gene that carries it. I know of relatives who inherited the double dose who suffer from the disease and others who have passed away because of it. To look on the bright side, the trait gives some protection against severe malaria.

After the internship, as there was a training job going in microbiology, I decided to go for it. Why microbiology? Well, infectious diseases are still very prevalent in developing countries. I thought this would be fertile ground for a successful career. I embarked on a three-year master of medicine (MMed) pathology course with microbiology as my specialty. The first year entailed a rotation in the other specialties of pathology, namely haematology, clinical chemistry and histopathology. Professor Owor was the head of histopathology during the three month I was in that department. I had such a wonderful time there that I was almost persuaded to pursue a career in histopathology. Looking back now, histopathologists had well defined roles compared with clinical microbiologists whose roles are sometimes poorly defined. Take the example of a good and experienced biomedical scientist who can do many duties of a medical microbiologist. The same goes for infection control practitioners. On balance, I do not regret choosing microbiology as performing a wide range of duties was quite exciting. The other thing is that there is nothing wrong with sharing duties with other professional as long as their intentions are honourable.

6

I Meet my Mentor

I was sitting in the corridor near Dr Hathaway's office nervously looking at the door and occasionally glancing at my watch to check the time. Dr Hathaway, a Canadian immunologist, was the head of the microbiology service. She had made arrangements for me to meet Dr Robert Blowers who was visiting Uganda as an external examiner. I had embarked on a master of medicine (MMed) Pathology postgraduate course that required rotation in the four departments of pathology namely cellular pathology, clinical biochemistry, haematology and microbiology. I had gone through the first three departments and I was now in microbiology, the speciality I was going to concentrate on. That's why I was nick-named 'Bugs doctor' –the bug as in the bacteria or microorganism sense. Being an immunologist, Dr Hathaway could not supervise my training. The plan was to do a diploma in bacteriology in Manchester and then return to Uganda to complete my Master of Medicine (MMed) course. One of the requirements for registering for the diploma course was spending a year in a recognised laboratory in the UK. I was now waiting to request that Dr Blowers allow me to spend the year in his laboratory at Northwick Park Hospital.

The door opened and Dr Hathaway waved her hand, 'Come in Emmanuel, Dr Blowers is ready to see you'. I walked in and saw this smiling middle-aged man extending his hand to me and saying, 'Hello Emmanuel, What can I do for you?' He gave me quite a firm handshake and showed me to the chair. He and Dr Hathaway remained standing. I explained what I wanted. I had never had an easier and more comfortable interview. He

jotted down a few words and said.' I think I can be of some help'.
I had met my mentor.

That reminds me of another related subject of role models
whose aspects of their life, particularly success, are emulated by
people especially the young. Other aspects include hard work,
honesty and tolerance among many others. It is not easy to find
an 'all in one' role model. That is why many people are disappointed when it is revealed that a role model has shortcomings.
This is because they expected an 'all in one' role model or confuse
success with perfection. My attitudes on this issue have evolved
over the years. I came to a conclusion that role modelling is
activity or character specific.

Going back to my mentor Dr Blowers, the next time I saw
him was in his large office at Northwick Park hospital in the UK.

7

My Training at
Northwick Park Hospital

I arrived in the UK mid October 1975. The weather was getting rather cold but this was no problem as I padded myself with a thick winter coat and a pair of warm gloves. I virtually landed running.

My primary goal was to gather as much knowledge as possible in preparation for the diploma in bacteriology in Manchester in 1976. I spent a lot of time on the laboratory bench shadowing biomedical scientists. I worked closely with all grades of biomedical scientists. I remember one biomedical scientist, a lady called Jenny Stirling, who kept a close eye on what was going on in the main laboratory. She would spend time at reception picking out specimens that required special attention as assessed by the clinical information given. Other senior members of staff like Mike Vogler and Devendra Kothari worked in the 'Serology Unit'. Unlike the main laboratory where live organisms were isolated, in serology, antibodies to the causative organisms or parts of them (called antigens) were detected in blood specimens. Working with them, gave me an insight of how these highly professional people run a diagnostic laboratory efficiently. They processed specimens and produced reports. The results were put into the computer. At the time in the mid-1970s, the use of computers in laboratories was still in its infancy. The data entry was by a punch card system. The printed reports had to be checked for accuracy and relevancy to the clinical information given by the clinicians. This task was performed by the medical staff in the department. The senior registrar at the time was a very amicable Dr Jobanaputra. His main job was to authorise the reports. I spent quite a lot of time with him learning the skill of authorising reports.

As head of department and my mentor, Dr Blowers taught me a lot on infection control matters for which he was internationally renowned. I accompanied him to operating theatres to perform air sampling for assessing bacterial contamination of air.

I also spent some time in the sterilisation department to learn more about autoclaves. This was an important part of my training because these machines are used to sterilise theatre instruments and linen as well as decontamination of clinical waste, which may have dangerous pathogens.

Dr Blowers gave a lot of advice on numerous topics in microbiology and infection control. One afternoon, Dr Blowers was giving me a tutorial in his office when the senior clinician virtually burst in with Dr Blower's secretary behind with an 'I could not stop him' expression on her face.

'Bob, how do you treat...?', he asked almost out of breath.

Dr Blowers calmly replied, 'I'm not really sure. I will check and come back to you'.

When the clinician had left, he turned to me and said, 'You don't have to give an answer if you are not sure'. I stuck to that advice for the rest of my career. I kept in touch with him. In fact in the summer of 1985, he and his wife Gethin paid us a visit at our home in Canterbury.

I also had the pleasure of working with Dr Keith Rogers a veteran microbiologist who had worked with Alexander Fleming (the discoverer of penicillin) at St Mary's Hospital, Paddington. Dr Rogers, a softly spoken gentleman – a real gentleman, always carried a hand lens in the pocket of his laboratory coat. As soon as he was shown any culture by the laboratory staff, he would whip out the hand lens and closely examine the culture. He would say, 'this is likely to be Streptococcus Group A-the colony is quite dry'. On another occasion, he would say, 'Look, the colony has little feet – it is likely to be Candida'.

At around 11 am, the medical staff did what we called a 'milk round' going round the benches to collect the results 'hot off the press' so that we would advise the clinician as soon as possible. We would jokingly put 'bets' of 10p on the likely identity of a culture. All this was valuable experience for me.

Later on, Dr Philip Sanderson became the head of the department while Dr Blowers spent more time doing research on infection control, particularly on operating theatres. Dr Sanderson was a very competent microbiologist. He was a prolific writer of review articles. One of the important things he taught me was to add comments to reports – He talked about adding 'guarded comments' to reports. He was the first generation of microbiologists to go to the wards to see patients. We frequently visited the intensive care unit. This was the beginning of my interest in intensive care patients.

The isolation unit at Northwick Park was one of the best in the country at the time. Every Thursday morning, I was part of the microbiology delegation including biomedical scientists like Devendra Kothari to go to attend a ward round on the isolation unit. I met wonderful and knowledgeable people like Dr Larson, a tall American, who was one the authors of the paper describing the first case of Clostridium difficile infection. Soon after every ward round, he led reviews of the weekly Communicable Disease Report (CDR), which was a UK publication and the Morbidity and Mortality Report (from US). The CDR was compiled from submissions of interesting cases sent in by hundreds of laboratories to the Central Public Health Laboratory at Colindale near London. If the reported infection was very unique, the name of reporting laboratory would be mentioned. It was a source of pride to see the name of ones laboratory in the report. These were truly the 'good old days' before the advent of seeking financial gain for every activity performed.

There were other prominent infectious disease specialists on these ward rounds –they included Dr David Tyrrell who did a lot of work on the common cold and Dr Hillas Smith a very experienced physician. It was on such occasion, I met Dr Kabuubi a fellow Ugandan. When he introduced himself, I recognised the tribal name. I responded by saying, 'Wasuze otyano sebo' meaning

'Good morning sir'. His facial expression of surprise was amazing. We remained in touch for many years until he joined the army and went abroad.

In 1976, the political situation back home in Uganda was getting really bad. The University, from which I was receiving financial support, wrote stating that it was no longer possible to send funds for my maintenance and that I had to go back immediately. My plans for the diploma were shattered. I explained my dilemma to my mentor and Dr Sanderson who advised me to embark on the Royal College of Pathologists' membership five-year course. I will always be grateful for their understanding and support at that very difficult time. I was lucky to pass the primary membership examination in 1977. Later that year when Dr Jobanputra was appointed consultant microbiologist at Peterborough, I applied for the vacant job of senior registrar and got it. This was wonderful as it was now possible for our three-year-old son Bobby to join us in our first home in Harrow Weald.

In order to gain the experience of working in another laboratory, when the job of lecturer was advertised at the Middlesex hospital, I applied and got it. I did not have to move house but I had a bit of commuting to do. I walked, took a bus, then underground train and then walked again. It was a good physical exercise.

At Middlesex hospital medical school, I met a very interesting Dr John Holton. He had vast knowledge of microbiology. We nicknamed him 'the walking encyclopaedia'. In June 1981, we both passed the final examination of the Royal College of Pathologists. I became a Member of the Royal College of Pathologist (MRCPath.) and three months later, I applied and got the job of consultant microbiologist in Canterbury and Thanet Health District.

8

My Encounter with HIV/AIDS

One morning in the early 1980s, Dr Hussein a consultant psychiatrist came to my office. He said that he had brought in a specimen and had decided to have a quick chat with me. We had the usual conversation about work, our families and after a while he got up and headed for the door. He suddenly turned and asked, 'what is this new syndrome I have just read about AIDS? What is it?' I invited him to sit down again, pointing to the chair he had been sitting on. I told him the little I knew about it at the time and what it stood for – that is 'Acquired Immune Deficiency Syndrome'.

'You know more than I do', he said as he got up. He invited me to give his group a talk at one of their lunchtime meetings.

A few weeks later, I gave my first talk on the subject. I mentioned its association with Kaposi Sarcoma and other probable associations we knew at the time. The cause was not known then. Soon after that a candidate virus was announced – HTLV3.

Around that time, a brilliant young man was appointed as consultant haematologist with an interest in haemophilia. His name was Mark Winter. He had diagnosed many cases among his haemophilia patients. He had first-hand experience of the condition and he started giving many lectures to health care staff in the area. It soon became established that this was a blood borne virus. Eventually it was identified as HIV (Human Immunodeficiency Virus).

My main contribution was formulation of the infection control guidelines under the big umbrella 'Blood borne viruses'.

Like other blood borne viruses, for example Hepatitis B, it was soon established that HIV too, was sexually transmitted.

In the late 1980s, HIV/AIDS became a major problem in the Ugandan diaspora. I was asked to give talks at social gatherings on the mode of transmission and preventive measures. The emphasis was on behavioural change. I also emphasised personal responsibility and having the right mind set of long term ambitions of surviving to see their children graduating from college, getting married and so on.

In the 1990s a lot of work was done in improving the laboratory tests. My own department and the department of biochemistry worked together to introduce the 'same day testing' meaning that the patients were able to get results on the same day. Working with the Department of biochemistry was quite easy because it was headed by a colleague and friend of mine Dr Paul Buamah who on retirement in 2005 returned to Ghana to open his own private hospital.

As most people know, the main breakthrough in the management of HIV/AIDS came with the introductions of anti-retroviral drugs. Hitherto, a lot of laboratory effort and resources were spent on the diagnosis and management of opportunistic infections. These were infections, which took advantage of a weakened body and caused havoc. All this changed with the advent of the antiretroviral.

As the person responsible for formulating the antimicrobial guidelines, I had also to formulate the guidelines for anti-retroviral. I did this job for quite a while until the department of Genitourinary Medicine took over this responsibility. This coincided with the Public Health Laboratory Service (PHLS) taking over the management of the microbiology services in East Kent in 2001.

In July 2004, I attended the XV International HIV/AIDS Conference in Bangkok, Thailand. Talking to and listening to experts and delegates from different parts of the world indicated that the virus was indeed a global problem, which required international effort to control its spread. President Nelson Mandela of South Africa was one of the dignitaries who spoke to the delegates.

By the time I retired in 2012, I had very little role to play in the management of this important infection. We still had the occasional case admitted with full – blown AIDS. The current plea to the public to get tested and start early treatment is as valid now as it was those many years ago.

To commemorate World AIDS Day on 1 December 2004, my son Paulo Ndawula wrote an impressive song entitled *'Don't Pass It On'* which emphasises the role of personal responsibility in preventing the spread of HIV.

9

I Made Them Sleepy:
I Also Excited Them

I always spent a lot of time preparing my lectures. If it was the first lecture, I would gather material and plan for weeks. They were however tailor-made for each audience.

It was a warm Wednesday afternoon. I had come to the lecture room some twenty minutes before the lecture was due to start to make sure that all the equipment was in good working order. Soon the room was almost full. 'How many more do we expect?' I asked.

'A few of our colleagues are on call – they will not be coming', replied one the young doctors sitting in the front row.

'Good afternoon, my name is...,' I started the talk. Ten minutes later, I noticed that a few of those at the back were dosing off. As most lecturers know, this was a very uncomfortable situation. I raised my voice to emphasize the point I was making. That temporarily did the trick for some minutes but a few moments later; a few more had joined them in the slumber land. I was really relieved when I came to the bit 'in summary...'. To my surprise, the post-lecture assessment was very good.

A year later at the same venue, the same lecture, different group and not a single person dosed off. The enthusiasm was palpable and the interaction was fantastic. One week later, I went to the postgraduate office to check on post lecture assessment. The majority gave 'excellent'. In fact one of the young doctors awarded 15 out of 10! That really touched me. The immediate benefit of a well-attended and received talk was that I would get less calls asking for advice. The long-term benefit is the good training for the future practitioners.

Months later, I was walking along a hospital corridor when I heard a familiar voice behind me calling my name. I stopped and looked back. It was one of the senior consultant surgeons. He said, 'that lecture you gave on Hepatitis B was excellent. This is the first time I really understood hepatitis B'. I thanked him for the compliment. As I walked on, I felt a real spring in my step. Such little things make the job worthwhile.

The other exciting thing is the wide range of health care staff I have given talks to over the years. They included nurses, pharmacists, ambulance staff, and physiotherapists to mention but a few. Each lecture was tailor-made for a particular group and the prevailing 'newsworthy' pathogens.

The vast number of topics was continuously changing because the three interacting components of infection and its management, namely the causative pathogens, the people they infect and the antimicrobial drugs used are constantly changing. As a consequence, there was this urge to pass on new exciting information to the users of the service. My favourite topic was, 'The rational use of antimicrobial drugs'

The evolution of visual aids I used over the years is worth a mention. I did not use a blackboard, which my teachers used in my primary, secondary and medical school. Technology had improved but not very much. I acquired a small projector with a round carousel for housing the slides. The first slides I used were made of thin glass, which easily broke with the slightest pressure. Then we moved on to those made of plastic. All the while, the department of medical illustration was invaluable to me. One outstanding person who did a lot of my work was Mrs Jill Fell. Before long, the day of PowerPoint arrived and visual aids changed beyond recognition.

10

The Power of Putting Pen to Paper

It was four o'clock in the afternoon. My secretary, Gina Potter walked into my office with a letter she had just typed. She put it on the table and waited for me to read through and sign it so as not to miss the end of day post. The letter was to a surgeon who was not adhering to our guidelines of giving only one dose of antibiotic just before performing a particular type of operation. He was giving three doses – one before the operation and two more afterwards. Signing the letter was the easy bit. I had done a lot of work putting that letter together – quoting our guidelines and additional references indicating that one dose was effective in preventing post operation infections for the type of operation. I signed it and off it went. A few days later, our infection control team reported back to me that the surgeon was complying with our guidelines. I was over the moon; the power of the pen had worked. This was one of hundreds of occasions I had used this weapon. Writing letters to colleagues had a personal and professional touch. With advent of e-mails, the number letters I wrote on some subjects went down. I had to improve my typing skills.

Formulating guidelines was one of the ways I put the written word to effective use. To achieve the desired goal, they had to be good and well-written documents. I spent a lot of time collecting evidence for the contents as well as involving the target groups for them to be true stakeholders. The results were satisfying, as happened in one instance when I sent out guidelines on 'The prevention of infections in patients that had undergone splenectomies (lost their spleens)'. I received a response from a surgeon by the name of Peter Pheils – a tall man with a big heart. His response was one word 'Exemplary'. That touched me. I felt that all that effort was worth it. Most of all, I knew that if the guidelines were correctly followed, serious infections would be prevented. The most common of these infections is caused by an organism called Pneumococcus. It causes pneumonia and meningitis, both of which can be accompanied by septicaemia (blood poisoning). People with no spleens or those who have dysfunctional spleens are susceptible to these infections. They can be prevented by giving prophylactic antibiotics and/or vaccination. Details of these were given in the guidelines, which Peter Pheils read and appreciated.

Over the years, I formulated many guidelines covering a variety of topics including laundry, disinfectants, mattresses, antibiotics, HIV and hepatitis viruses to name but a few. I also formulated guidelines for very rare but deadly infections for example viral haemorrhagic fevers including Ebola, Marburg and Lassa. The reason for this was that if a suspected case arrived in casualty, we would be ready with the necessary equipment and protective clothing to prevent spread. We did not wait for the department of health to remind us of our responsibilities. We kept abreast all legislations and national guidelines. I must mention and thank the person who did most of the typing and document management. Her name was Tina Dunstall and was based at Margate.

The amount of effort I put in to produce the guidelines was worthwhile, as I knew that they contributed to better patient care. We used them as standards for clinical audit, which is a very important tool in improving the quality of care. They all proved the power of the written word. The rare occasions when the medico legal issues were raised, the written word was very useful.

In order to achieve uniformity of performing tests, the laboratory had clear written instructions for each test. We called these standard operating procedures (SOPs). As head of service, it was my responsibility to approve them and to make sure that they were up to date. We had an SOP for almost everything.

In fact, we used to joke about having an SOP for even sitting on a chair! Joking apart, in addition to SOPs, within the department we had protocols, rules and policies. All the four had one thing in common: they were mandatory. Any deviation from them was regarded as a violation, which was a serious matter. As a service department, we formulated guidelines to other departments in the rest of the hospital and as such were not mandatory. However, heads of service could make them mandatory in their own departments if they so wished.

One the most important aspect of managing guidelines is making sure that there are not many versions of them in circulation at the same time leading to confusion among the users. This can also happen when the users are constantly bombarded with articles from literature on the same topic. New information should be put in the next version of the guidelines. It is also very tempting for the authors of guidelines to include information of special interest to the author but not necessarily relevant to theme of the guidelines.

11

Meetings That Made a Difference and Those That Were a Bit of Damp Squib

It was a warm Friday afternoon on 7 July 1995 when I entered the small Pharmacy seminar room carrying documents for the meeting I was about to chair. A few people had already gathered. They were members of the Kent and Canterbury Infection Control Committee. As chairman, I sat at the head of the table. Next to me was Linda Dempster, the infection control nurse. After a few usual remarks on the weather, I took the documents out of my brown folder and started arranging them in the order of the agenda. Within minutes the room was almost full. I looked at my watch – It was a minute to two o'clock, the scheduled start of the meeting. I was about to open my mouth, when the last person burst in and took his seat. They were all punctual.

'Welcome everybody,' was my opening remark. I was the chairman and the secretary of the meeting. Linda also helped me to take some notes. As soon as the meeting was over, we compared notes and then I went straight back to my office and jotted down all the details ready for typing by the secretary on Monday. I was at pains to make sure that the minutes were a true record of the meeting. Years later when we referred to them, we would know who said what, who did what, how decisions were made and how problems were solved. At one time, hospital management tried to standardise the format of minutes to bullet points. Reading these, one would not tell who said what, not to mention all other important details. Needless to say, I was not happy with the changes. In the meantime, I was glad it was Friday and we were coming to the end of a busy week.

Earlier in the week, I had chaired a similar meeting of the Thanet Infection Control Committee. This belonged to another Trust. Therefore, you can say that I was serving two masters. It was a tiring exercise, but enjoyable and satisfying because I knew that the work had tangible benefits to patients.

A few days before the Thanet meeting, I had chaired a laboratory meeting, which was very technical and was mainly about laboratory methods. The good thing about the meeting was that all laboratory staff were invited. I remember encouraging the quietest member of staff to make a contribution to the discussion because I had heard through the grape vine that she had a brilliant idea on one agenda topic.

The Drugs and Therapeutics Committee, as the title suggests was concerned with formulating policies and guidelines on safe prescribing of drugs. It was responsible for overseeing the introduction of new drugs. To that end, pharmacists on the committee collected all the relevant information on the drugs that were to be approved by the committee. I was always impressed by the professional way they presented the information to the committee. For the sake of transparency and to avoid conflicts of interest, one constant agenda item was the declaration of interest by the members. Two chairmen of this committee stood out for their service – Dr Don Prosser, who was renal physician and Dr Michael Jenkinson – a care of the elderly physician. I served on this committee because of my expertise on antimicrobial drugs. I did this continuously for thirty years, seventeen of which I had no choice as I was the only consultant microbiologist in the health district of a population of 300,000.

Another committee, I enjoyed serving on was the Clinical Services Committee of the Association of Medical Microbiologists. For four years from 1995 to 1999, I represented the South East Regional Microbiology Subcommittee on this national committee. I had a chance to meet regularly with microbiologists from all over the UK. This was a committee from which I took clear messages of good practice back to the group I represented and to my own department.

The above mentioned are few examples of effective committees I had the pleasure of serving on. They shared several features. All the chairmen and members worked hard before, during and after the meetings. Their committee work was part and parcel of the work they were trained to do in their specialty. The skills needed to do their committee work improved as time went on. For chairmen, they were the skills of interpersonal communication and listening. For members, they were the skills of communicating effectively in their areas of expertise. Their committee work formed a small proportion of their day-to-day work.

The other meetings of committees I attended were the opposite of what I have just described. At one of such meetings, the chairman would come in late and without any documents. He had to borrow my agenda and minutes of the last meeting. As the meeting went on aimlessly, one or people dominated the proceedings while others lost interest and started side conversations. At the end of an agenda item, there was no clear decision: instead, the chairman said that the issue would be discussed outside the meeting by a smaller group of members. This was quite a common occurrence at some of these meetings. As I had prepared for a meeting, I would make an attempt to make a contribution to the discussion. When the minutes were sent out, I was always shocked to find that they bore little resemblance to what happened at the meeting. It was quite common for my contributions to be completely omitted. It was also as if the minutes had been manipulated to suit the chairman and the parent group to which the minutes were sent. I was not alone to have this experience. Many other people complained privately and publically but in vain.

Two reasons why I went to work very early in the morning were to avoid the morning traffic and to find a parking space. If I was delayed for any reason, it was almost impossible to find a parking space in areas allocated for health care staff. Then I would be condemned to driving round and round the hospital looking for that elusive parking space. I knew for sure that the clinical activities had not dramatically increased. The other change I noticed was that it was becoming increasingly difficult to find a room, any room, to hold a meeting. I also noticed that when I tried to contact some colleagues on clinical matters, their medical secretaries would inform me that they were at meetings. From these observations, I came to a conclusion that the number of meetings had really increased.

This opens up the discussion on the role of the increasing committee work in the provision of health services. To put things in perspective, I always look at other professionals outside the health service. Take professional tennis players as an example. Their day at the office is marked by long hours of practice and playing matches. Their professional development is assessed by winning matches and tournaments, which affect their ranking. Let us take another example – that of a concert pianist who also does a lot of practice. Years of this improves his/her performance to the delight of audiences.

Returning to the health service, there are some specialties in which professionals have very clearly defined roles, for example surgery. The main duty of a surgeon is to perform operations and like a concert pianist, practice will turn him or her into an accomplished performer. Doctors, however, have other duties, which are part of good practice. These include research, clinical audit, teaching and management to mention but a few. Even with these, a person doing research for example should not spend a lot of time at meetings. Most of his/her time should be spent performing research, reviewing literature and publishing papers, which will be the final evidence of their work. That is why there was once a saying, 'Publish or perish'. The results of the other activities like clinical audit should be there for all to see and assess. Meetings have become the dominant activities for some health care staff. I would not be surprised to know that some senior health care professionals these days on returning home to their loved ones would say, 'My day at the office was a series of committee meetings'.

The general public can assess the performance of a tennis player by the quality of the passing shot or drop shot but cannot easily do that for a person who looks after their health. Maybe one day a patient will make enquiries about how much time a specialist spends on committee work in comparison to direct patient care under the heading of 'Patient choice'.

During the process of looking for the best doctor, the notion of 'practice makes perfect' should not be lost on a patient seeking treatment for a serious condition. Take two surgeons who have been consultants for ten years. One, who has been a senior manager for four years, performs the occasional operation and spends most of his time attending meetings. On the contrary, the other surgeon spends most of his time performing operations. Who should the patient choose to operate on him/her? If the rule of 'money follows patients' was applied, who should be paid more?

As the cost of health care is scrutinised more and more, the quality of committee work should also be looked at more closely. Taxpayers may not be aware of this important activity.

12

My Special Relationship with General Practitioners

One of the GPs in the Margate area frequently phoned me asking for advice on a wide range of issues. After one of these conversations, out of the blue, she invited me to give a talk to GPs in her group on a topic of my choice. I accepted and chose to give a talk entitled, 'Making the best use of the microbiology laboratory'. I gave the talk on 12 May 2011. I concentrated on the type of specimen recommended for various infections and the interpretation of results. The talk went very well – at least that is what they told me. The GP who invited me never phoned again until I retired a year later. That was the last lecture I gave to GPs.

Over the years, I had given many talks to the GPs. The first set of talks was to 'medical societies'. A group of GPs in a locality formed a medical society. It was common practice at the time for a medical society to invite a newly appointed consultant to give a talk to them. I gave the very first one in 1982 to the Ramsgate Medical Society. I was rather nervous because I was new to the area and I had not talked to such a forum before. It was on the same theme as the above-mentioned talk – the use of microbiology services. I need not have worried as they welcomed me warmly. The interactive talk and questions that followed went smoothly.

For many years, as the only medical microbiologist in the health authority area, I had to participate in many GP training programmes. This was of mutual benefit to me and the GPs. I became aware of their needs and I informed them of what the laboratory could offer. The two services were closely linked with no 'middlemen' and this improved patient care. It was a patient-GP-microbiologist axis. This was pure and simple.

In 1994, I formulated a booklet '*A guide to using the laboratory*' for all laboratory users including GPs. The booklet consisted of many types of infections; the type of specimen required for each; the tests to be requested and comments about those tests. It also included 'Turn-around times' which is the time between sending the specimen and receiving the results. For microbiology results, this ranges from the same day to several weeks. It also had a format of a typical report explaining the terms used on the report.

The following year, I issued another booklet entitled '*Antimicrobial Guidelines for General Practitioners*' which had introductory remarks of the rational use of antibiotics and treatments for more than fifty common conditions.

Over the years I tried to help GPs in the investigation, treatment and prevention of infections. For seventeen years (from 1982 to 1999), as a single-handed microbiologist, I provided a microbiology service to a large number of GPs. The service took many forms.

The two laboratories at Canterbury and Margate processed a large number of specimens from GPs. The requested tests on these specimens varied in complexity. We even occasionally received ticks and worms for identification; it was always exciting for me to confirm a diagnosis for a doctor who mentioned a provisional diagnosis on the request form. After isolating the causative organism, I would gladly add a comment 'This confirms the diagnosis of such and such infection'. Occasionally I bumped into one of these GPs and they would say 'Hey, thank you for that report' and I would return the compliment by saying 'Thank you for the accurate spot diagnosis'. That always made my day.

Providing survey data is another service I provided to GPs every year without fail. This involved compiling all the organisms isolated from one type of specimen together with their susceptibility test results to various antibiotics. In cases of urinary tract infection, it would be organisms isolated from urine specimens. I worked out the percentages of organisms that were sensitive to a particular antibiotic. This would enable the GPs to estimate the chances of effective treatment when they started a patient on a particular antibiotic before they received the results of the specimen, or if they did not send any specimen. This also helped us in looking at trends in the susceptibility of the pathogens to antibiotics in our local population.

In addition, I gave a list of pathogens isolated from stools of patients who presented with diarrhoea. The list would include pathogens like Campylobacter (the commonest bacterial cause of food poisoning), Salmonella as well as viruses like Rotavirus which cause diarrhoea in children. I wrote short notes on the interesting pathogens. This data was sent to more than two hundred GPs in my catchment area. This was useful to them but also encouraged those who were not keen to send specimens to start sending more specimens. The annual data was sent out every January for seventeen years. It is a practice l enjoyed doing for my favourite group of doctors. I had and still have a special admiration for GPs, for their mental agility in that a GP would be dealing with a ninety-year-old man one minute, a toddler in the next and a teenager after that.

13

The Real McCoy

My office was very cold that morning. The radiators were not working. I phoned the works department to send down a man to look at them and I was expecting him any moment. There was a knock at the door. When I said 'Come in', I was expecting to see a man from the works department. Instead it was Dave Bissessur, the senior biomedical scientist. 'Doctor, we got it spot on', he said with excitement as he showed me a piece of paper he was holding. 'The NEQAS Gentamicin results are back,' he continued. 'Look our result is 2.1 and the expected result is 2.1', he said as he fingered the two numbers in front of my face.

'Wonderful' I responded with matching enthusiasm.

I better explain what we were talking about. Gentamicin is a useful antibiotic but if not used properly can be toxic to the kidneys and parts of the ear. It can cause conversational hearing loss, loss of balance and ringing in ears. The dose for effective treatment is very close to the dose that can cause toxicity. It is therefore good laboratory practice to monitor the blood levels of the drug to make sure that the patient on Gentamicin is getting enough drug for effective treatment and not too much to suffer the toxic effects of the drug. How does the laboratory know that it is doing a good job in monitoring the blood levels of the drug? Better still, how is the patient reassured that the blood level monitoring is accurate? That is how the UK NEQAS comes into the picture.

The UK National External Quality Assessment Service (UK NEQAS) is a very important organisation for assessing the quality of services provided by laboratories. It provides

45

laboratories with simulated specimens with relevant clinical information. The laboratories are supposed to process these specimens in the same way they treat the specimens from patients. The results are returned to UK NEQAS for assessment. Poor performers are helped to improve through education and advice by UK NEQAS.

For years, I had a special interest in the laboratory diagnosis of parasitic infections. The gut parasitic infections are detected by microscopic examination of faecal samples. I was always delighted when the technical staff asked me for a second opinion on a parasite they were not sure of. This included simulated NEQAS specimens, some of which had very exotic parasites, which we hardly come across in the routine work. This made the examination of this specimen very exciting. We did not deal with the blood parasites like malaria, as these were investigated by the department of haematology.

Laboratories also monitor the quality of their work through schemes of internal quality control. In early 1980s, I remember spending a lot of time in the laboratory trying to find out the best media for isolating certain types of organisms called Streptococci that cause sore throat. These organisms exhibit a characteristic appearance on the solid culture media. The meticulous work I was doing, most of it in the evenings when other staff had gone home, was to select the media on which the organism would easily be recognised. What this meant was that if a doctor sent a throat swab from a child with a sore throat, the causative organism would not be missed. That child would then get the correct treatment.

A friend of mine living in another part of the country contacted me concerning a skin condition he had. He had been referred to a dermatologist who made a diagnosis of Pityriasis vesicolor. A specimen in the form of skin scrapings was sent to a nearby laboratory. His condition improved on the medication he was given. He went to see his GP on another matter; he thought he could as well inquire about the results of the skin specimen. The GP turned the computer monitor to him so that he could read for himself. My friend took out a piece of paper and wrote it down. The GP told him that it was a negative result. Later on that day when he phoned me, he read it out, 'Microscopy: Fungal elements not seen. Culture: Fungi not isolated'. So he asked me 'What does that mean?'

I explained, 'Pityriasis versicolor is caused by a fungus called Malassezia furfur. The laboratory diagnosis is made by looking at a good skin specimen under a microscope- a process called microscopy and seeing structures which look like spaghetti and meatballs. To grow the fungus, a special fatty media is required. Most laboratories do not have this media and therefore do not isolate the fungus.'

What does this story have to do with quality of service? The ideal management of my friend's condition would be to have a good GP who, when not sure, would refer him to a good dermatologist who would make the correct diagnosis which he would write on the request form accompanying a correctly taken specimen. In the laboratory, the specimen would be processed by well-trained biomedical scientists who would put extra effort on microscopy. The results would be presented to a consultant medical microbiologist, like me, who should be familiar with this condition and would know the limitations of the laboratory methods. He/she would add a comment like this 'A negative result does not rule out the diagnosis of Pityriasis versicolor as this laboratory does not routinely use a special media for this fungus'. If my friend had read a comment like this, he would not have contacted me to ask, 'What does that mean?' That is what quality is about. That is the real McCoy.

The story of my friend demonstrates the three phases of a laboratory test. The first, being the pre-analytical phase, entails what the clinician writes on the request form, the quality of the specimen and the time it takes to reach the laboratory. The laboratory should issue clear guidelines for the clinician on the type of specimen required for a particular condition, and how to transport it safely to the laboratory. Some infections are caused by very delicate organisms, which need special transport media to keep them viable by the time the specimen arrives in the laboratory. Delays in transit can affect the viability of such organisms. The second is the analytical phase, which is the actual processing of the specimens by the biomedical scientists. The last one is the post-analytical phase, which entails the interpretation of the results and their delivery to the requesting doctors and other practitioners in a timely manner. It may be necessary to telephone some results especially in cases that need urgent treatment. Patients should assess the quality of the laboratory tests by looking critically at all the three phases; after all they pay for them directly or through taxation.

One other way of improving the quality of work of a service department is liaising with another service department. As an example, if a clinician was investigating a patient with non-pulmonary tuberculosis (not affecting the lungs), two specimens would normally be sent – one to histopathology and the other to microbiology. I would contact my colleagues in histopathology to compare our findings. One of the people I frequently contacted was my friend and colleague Dr Aminu Abdulkadir. Knowing people in other departments made the process much easier.

14

The Old Woman with a Nasty Leg Ulcer

It was Thursday afternoon. I had just come back to my office after visiting two patients on care of the elderly wards. They had Clostridium difficile infection, which at the time was a national media obsession and had to be managed well to prevent outbreaks like one that had badly affected a neighbouring hospital, resulting in very unfavourable press. These two patients also happened to have very bad leg ulcers for which I had just given some advice.

I started authorising reports. The first report on the queue was of a result of a swab from a leg ulcer of an 80-year-old woman. I remember mumbling to myself, 'they come in threes'. This was the third patient with a leg ulcer problem I had encountered within the hour. The leg ulcer swab had been sent in by a general practitioner who had given very good clinical information indicating that she had had this ulcer for over a year but of late it was producing a profuse green discharge. Previous swabs had shown no significant growth. The report I was looking at also had similar wording, 'No significant growth'. This was the interpretation of the biomedical scientist who produced the report. The supressed information revealed that an organism called Pseudomonas aeruginosa has been isolated. In fact on looking back at the previous reports, the same organism had been isolated. Obviously there was a clinical problem for which the GP was seeking help from the laboratory. I changed the report to indicate that Pseudomonas had been isolated and added a comment, '*This is of doubtful significance as Pseudomonas commonly colonises areas of broken skin especially of the lower limbs. I suggest cleaning with an antiseptic solution and covering the area with a good quality dressing (impermeable to bacteria; protecting the area from further contamination). The blue-green colour of the exudate is likely to be due to the presence of Pseudomonas aeruginosa colonizing the site*'.

There are many underlying problems of leg ulcers including diabetes and diseases of blood vessels. Chronic leg ulcers (because of their site) are invariably colonised (that is causing no tissue damage) or infected (tissue damaged). Heavy colonisation with low virulence organisms like Pseudomonas can cause a nasty discharge. They can also be infected with more virulent organisms like MRSA. If there are signs of infection, like the reddening of the skin around the ulcer, specimens should be sent to the microbiology laboratory to find the causative organism. To protect the ulcers from contamination or infection, use of a good dressing is recommended.

A few days later, I made a follow up call to her GP who informed me that the green discharge had disappeared and that the ulcer was healing. Antibiotics had not been prescribed.

Taking swabs from chronic leg ulcers had been a controversial subject of intense debate among microbiologists in our area of Kent and Medway. In fact it had been an agenda item for the group quarterly meetings for three years. The group had issued guidelines on the issue discouraging clinicians from sending swabs from chronic legs ulcers with a few clinical exceptions, which included patients whose host defences were weakened. In reality these were ill-defined; making it very difficult to implement. I was in a minority who thought that clinicians should send these specimens with good clinical information and that the laboratory should process the specimens, add comments relevant to the clinical information given, as well as the culture result. There was fear and mistrust that clinicians would overuse antibiotics on receiving the results of the specimens. It was my view that if clinicians are given reports with good comments, including clear statements that antibiotics should not be used in certain clinical situations, antibiotics were unlikely to be misused. This was an issue of trust in other people's professional integrity.

Most shoppers will identify with this. You buy a piece of equipment and on arriving home you find out that it is not working. You try to contact the shop by phone. You are offered options one to four before you can talk to anybody only to find that you had been connected to the wrong section of the shop. You are given another number to start the whole process again. I did not want any clinicians to go through that process of contacting the laboratory by phone because I had sent out an incomplete or ambiguous report. I strongly believed that a report should be so complete and meaningful that there is no need for a clinician to contact the laboratory for an interpretation. This usually happened when the clinician was with the patient whose report it was. I thought that this was very unfair for the clinician especially if he/she made an effort to give detailed clinical information on the request form or asked a specific question expecting an answer. Some colleagues had a different view. They often implied that incomplete reports encouraged the clinicians to contact the laboratory. There were problems with this approach. As the reports did not show the name of the person who authorised them; if the clinician contacted the laboratory seeking clarification of a report, the call may be put through to a microbiologist who did not authorise that particular report and was likely to know absolutely nothing about the report. The microbiologist who took the call would be put in an awkward position of trying to interpret a microbiology report, 'on the hoof'. Even if the clinician on the phone got the right person, the microbiologist might be on the ward in which case the interpretation was likely to be 'loose' and vague. I believed that the interpretation of the reports should be accurate and tight. By the way, professional dancers use the same adjectives to describe their dance.

Let me give a few more examples of some comments I used. Isolating two organisms – Group B Streptococcus and Staphylococcus aureus from a leg ulcer without any clinical information on the request form was quite common. The comment I usually added was 'Staphylococcus aureus is a recognised pathogen of skin and soft tissues. Group B streptococcus on the other hand commonly colonises ulcers of the lower limbs. Therefore it is of doubtful significance in this clinical setting'.

Isolating Staphylococcus intermedius from a wound would prompt the following comment; 'This is a zoonotic (acquired from dogs and cats) organism which has been associated with human disease'. I would also release a list of antibiotics that could be used if the clinician decided to treat. Occasionally, one came across an organism, which most clinician would not know. One such organism was Staphylococcus lugdunensis usually isolated from wounds. I would add this comment – 'Staphylococcus lugdunensis has been associated with serious infections similar to those caused by Staphylococcus aureus'.

I encountered a few instances when virulent organisms like Group A Streptococcus (nicknamed 'the flesh-eating bacteria' by the popular press) was isolated from a graft site soon after the operation. Clinical information given would usually be 'wound oozing slightly'. I would phone the doctors on the ward straight away or even go and see the patient if I was on site. If I discovered the patient was well, I would still start antibiotic treatment. I would add a comment, 'With a pathogen like Group A Streptococcus, even if the site is not yet infected it will soon be. I suggest pre-emptive therapy with one of the drugs listed'.

When pathogens like the ones I have just mentioned are first isolated from the specimen, sensitivity tests are performed to determine the best antibiotic to be used to treat the infection. This is usually done twenty-four hours after the arrival of the specimen in the laboratory and it will usually be another day before the report is sent out. On the report there is the name of the organism isolated and a list of antibiotics or using a more accurate term – antimicrobial drugs – each marked with letters – 'S' or 'R' or occasionally 'I'. S stands for 'Sensitive' – predicting effective therapy with normal doses of the drug. 'I' stands for intermediate sensitivity which means that effective therapy may be achieved with high doses of the drug and ' R' standing for 'resistant' which means that effective therapy is unlikely to be achieved even with high doses.

These terms remind me of funny instances when I would be talking to a young doctor about the sensitivities of an organism. The doctor would ask, 'What is he (referring to the patient) sensitive to?'

I would reply, 'The organism (putting emphasis on the word organism) is sensitive to…'. The question implied that the doctor wanted to kill the patient with the antibiotic!

What is not funny is the problem of people who are allergic to antimicrobial drugs especially a group of drugs called the 'β-lactams' of which Penicillin is a member. Clinical manifestations of allergy range from a rash to life threatening anaphylaxis. If there is a history of allergy to a drug, that drug must not be used for that individual. Alternatives should be sought. For some infections the alternatives to penicillin are 'Macrolides' of which Erythromycin and Clarithromycin are members. As if life is not complicated enough – some organisms are resistant to these as well. For these, Clindamycin would be the alternative. Interestingly, a small study I performed in 2005 with Helen Smith, a very capable Biomedical Scientist, showed that a few isolates of Group G Streptococci in our laboratory at Margate were also resistant to Clindamycin by a mechanism called 'inducible resistance' (a group of drugs inducing resistance in another group of drugs). Such instances are challenging for a microbiologist who has to find a suitable drug to treat the infection.

Going back to the reports, there are pathogens for which sensitivity tests are not routinely performed due to technical problems. For these, I added a comment, 'Sensitivity tests are not routinely performed for this organism. The available data suggests that the drug of choice is such and such'. For some pathogens like Campylobacter, which is the commonest bacterial cause of food poisoning in the UK, I went further and suggested the clinical scenarios in which the clinician should use the drug I had suggested but always adding a caution, 'assuming no contraindications' as the onus is on the attending doctor to check the safety profile of the drug being prescribed.

I found adding comments to reports very rewarding because it made clinicians aware of a person in the laboratory who was reading their clinical information and responding accordingly. A good report also empowers the patients to understand the type of infection they have, what caused it, and that they are getting appropriate treatment for it or indeed that they do not need an antibiotic for it. I would therefore encourage patients to get more information through their doctors about the microbiology reports of their specimens.

15

The Lorry Driver with a Headache

I checked my watch. It was 3.30 in the afternoon. It was time to do my ward round. As I headed for the door, the phone rang. 'Dr Ndawula, this is the SHO for Dr Rake. We came to see you this morning...' was a very excited voice at the end of the phone.

'Oh yes, I remember'. I responded.

He continued, 'Well, you were right the patient has endocarditis. We've just performed an ECHO, which showed vegetations. So what should we do?'

'Start therapy as given in the antibiotic guidelines. I will visit him tomorrow. I am at Margate at the moment', I said. I felt a glow of warmth as I put down the phone and saying, 'Yes' as I clenched my fist.

Six hours earlier, when I was in my office at Canterbury, Dr Mark Rake a consultant physician at the time and his team had come to see me. They told me a story of a forty-year-old lorry driver who had presented with a severe headache which had lasted for several days. He had intermittent fever and was feeling generally weak. They had done a lumbar puncture (to get cerebral spinal fluid – CSF) to rule out meningitis. They had also sent blood cultures to rule out septicaemia (blood poisoning). The CSF had shown the type of cells that were not typical of bacterial meningitis and had revealed no bacterial growth. The blood cultures of six out of six bottles had grown an organism, which had just been identified as Haemophilus aphrophilus. I had told Dr Rake and his team that the organism was a known cause of endocarditis (an infection of the endocardium – the inner layer of the heart, usually affecting the heart valves which are either native or artificial). In this patient, it was affecting the native valves. I added that it was notorious for satellite infections in other parts of the body including the brain. The ECHO (short for Echocardiogram – a test using sound waves to build up a detailed structure of the heart and how it is functioning) had just confirmed the diagnosis of Haemophilus aphrophilus endocarditis with small satellite infections to the brain probably causing the headaches. He was also anaemic which can be one of the features of endocarditis.

The following day I went to see the patient – a thin pale man who said that he had lost weight over the previous few weeks. Being on the right antibiotics, he made a good recovery and was discharged a few days later. This was an example of instances when the identity of an organism isolated from blood cultures points to a final diagnosis. The other examples include Streptococcus bovis, which is associated with lesions in the gut including cancer of the gut. The isolation of organisms like Streptococcus mitis, Streptococcus salivarius, Streptococcus sanguis and Streptococcus oralis all of which are residents of the mouth should ring alarm bells for the strong possibility of endocarditis.

I have cited the story of the lorry driver to make a point that people who come to hospital are from different backgrounds and occupations, which may or may not be relevant to their illness. In this case, it was not relevant.

Endocarditis is an example of conditions ending '-itis' meaning inflammation/infection of an organ or particular tissues. They include meningitis (membrane covering the brain), encephalitis (brain), lymphadenitis (lymph nodes), parotiditis (parotid gland), otitis externa (outer ear), otitis media (middle ear), conjunctivitis (lining of the inside of the eyelids and the white part of the eye), endolphthalmitis (whole eye), osteomyelitis (bone), tonsillitis (tonsils), laryngitis(larynx), epiglottitis (epiglottis), sinusitis (sinuses), mastitis (breasts), stomatitis (mouth and lips), oesophagitis (oesophagus) gastritis (stomach), gastroenteritis (stomach and small intestine), appendicitis (appendix), colitis (colon – large intestine), pancreatitis (pancreas), hepatitis (hepatocytes-liver cells) cholecystitis (gallbladder), peritonitis (peritoneum), cystitis (urinary bladder), pyelonephritis (kidneys), myositis (muscles), orchitis (testes), prostatitis (prostate), urethritis (urethra), salpingitis (fallopian tubes), endometritis (endometrium-inner membrane of the uterus), cervicitis (uterine cervix), fasciitis (fascia – a type of connective tissue that surround other tissues like muscles), arthritis (joints) and vasculitis (blood vessels) among others. The exceptions to the '-itis' rule include impetigo (skin), paronychia (skin along the edge of a nail) and pneumonia (lungs) among others. A micro-biologist should know all the causative organisms for these conditions, how to investigate them as well as being conversant with the antimicrobial drugs used to treat them. The right drug should reach a particular site in high enough concentrations to kill the causative organism. That is why it is very important to make the right diagnosis (see chapter 19 for more details). Patients should be told the diagnosis (which may be one of those I have listed above) so that they have confidence in the treatment process.

16

Beware of Mother Nature; If the Body Defences are Weakened.

One nice summer morning in June of 2002, I entered the intensive therapy unit to be greeted by, 'We've got a very interesting patient for you, bugs doctor'. We all went to the side room where the patient was. The consultant intensivist – the specialist in intensive care presented the case. A 40-year-old woman who originally came from the Far East had presented with a swinging temperature and haemoptysis (coughing blood). She had a history of pulmonary tuberculosis, which had been treated. Chest x-rays showed features of severe pneumonia, which required intensive care support. Relevant investigations including blood cultures were ordered. We put her on antibiotics, which after a few days did not make any difference to her clinical condition.

Days later I walked in ITU and declared, 'I have some interesting results on Ms X who is in the side room'. Penicillinium marneffei had been isolated from the blood cultures. This organism is a fungus, which was first isolated from bamboo rats in Vietnam. It is also found in soil in that part of the world. It causes infections in people whose host defences are weakened. The patient was also found to have HIV (see chapter 8). She was started on a prolonged course of antifungal drugs and made a slow but steady improvement under the care of the HIV specialists. She had recently returned for the Far East. She probably acquired the fungal infection during that visit.

Another related story was that of a man in his fifties who in the autumn of 2000, presented with fever and other signs of pneumonia. He also suffered from diabetes mellitus, which at the time was out of control. He too had returned from the Far East. We repeatedly isolated a gram-negative bacterium from his sputum and blood cultures. What do I mean by gram-negative bacterium? Let me pause and give a little bacteriology spill. According to what they look like after being treated with Gram stain (named after a Danish bacteriologist called Hans Christian Gram who devised the method in 1882), bacteria are put into two groups: those which look dark purple are called gram- positive and those that look pink are called gram- negative. Description of their shapes is also given, if they are round they are called cocci and if they are cylindrical they are called rods or bacilli. Going back to the patient, the organism that was isolated from him was a gram-negative rod, which we interpreted as the cause of his pneumonia. We treated him with the antibiotics according to the laboratory sensitivity tests. He did not improve. A breakthrough came when the organism was identified by the reference laboratory as Burkholderia pseudomallei. This organism is found in soil and water in the Far East and Northern Australia. It is the causative organism for melioidosis. The diagnosis of melioidosis in a diabetic patient was made. We went into more detailed history to ascertain the way he acquired the infection. He revealed that he had gone fishing on a few occasions, some of which were marked by torrential rain. We could not establish for sure how the organism got into his body but we knew that this organism causes severe infections in people whose defences are compromised. People with poorly controlled diabetes (and infections can cause this state) have defects in their host defences likely to be due to malfunctioning white blood cells, which revert to normality once the infection and diabetes are controlled. Burkholderia pseudomallei is one of those organisms for which laboratory tests cannot accurately predict the antibiotic of choice. For these types of organisms, we go by other peoples experience as given in medical literature. This is what we did for the patient and once we switched to the right antibiotic, he made a good recovery and was discharged from hospital.

This confirmed a little observation rule I had made about sensitivity tests: they are good predictors of effective therapy for infections caused by 'human' organisms (those normally residing on or in the human body) but poor predictors for effective therapy of infections caused by 'environmental' organisms like those found in soil. The latter organisms are also usually resistant to antibiotics because they live in 'tough neighbourhoods'; where they have 'learnt' to fend for themselves by developing resistance to naturally occurring antibacterial substances.

In January 1997, I remember having a long discussion with a medical registrar about an immunocompromised patient from whom we had isolated an organism called Mycobacterium avium-intracellulare, which was resistant to almost all antibiotics tested. I was advising him to use a combination of drugs, which we had reported as resistant. Understandably, it did not make sense to him. Eventually, he bought the concept of laboratory tests predicting clinical outcome for infections caused by some organisms and not for the particular organism we were discussing. The proof of the pudding was that the patient got better and the organism was eradicated.

The summary of all this is that there are 'environmental' organisms, which can cause infections in individuals whose host defences, are weakened. Healthcare staff and these individuals should be aware of the fact that Mother Nature is the source of these potential pathogens. We have to look at the evolution timescale of the two. Modern medicine has changed the evolution scale of humans as those with very poor defences survive, thus disobeying Darwin's laws on natural selection. The microorganisms' environment is on a different scale in which they can adapt within hours of exposure to a hostile environment, therefore becoming a formidable enemy to us.

There are many infections that can be acquired from soil but people should not be unduly worried about catching nasty infections as they go about their daily activities like gardening. The examples I have given are those people whose body defences were weakened and went to areas of the world where these organisms are in soil. History of travel is very important when a person presents with a puzzling illness. Doctors should ask about such history. Tell them anyway in case they forget to ask.

17

Instances when Foreign Meant Trouble

O ne February morning 2002, I had just walked into my office, when Dave Bissessur, one of the senior Biomedical Scientist, virtually burst in the office saying, 'eight of eight positive with gram positive rods – they look like Diphtheroids.'

'Thank you Dave, leave the patient's details with me. I will deal with it straight away,' I said as I lifted the handset of the phone ready to dial. That was our jargon concerning blood cultures. When septicaemia (blood poisoning by bacteria) is suspected, this serious condition is investigated by taking blood cultures. This involves collecting blood from the patient and putting it in two bottles each containing a different type of media, (food for bacteria) one of which allows the growth of organisms that cannot tolerate oxygen. These organisms are known as anaerobes. The two bottles form a set, which is adequate for most causes of septicaemia. Serious conditions like endocarditis (infection of heart valves) need more than two sets for the proper interpretation of results.

From this patient four sets (eight bottles) were sent. This was a forty-five-year-old man with artificial heart valves. We later confirmed the diagnosis of artificial heart valve endocarditis. He was transferred to St Thomas Hospital for an operation to remove the infected valves. The causative organism was identified as Corynebacterium. 'Diphtheroids' is microbiology 'slang' for Corynebacterium species. They are skin organisms with low virulence but, in presence of a foreign material in the body, can cause infection. They are 'opportunists' that take advantage of compromised host defences. Foreign bodies do compromise the host defences. The other skin organisms notorious for causing opportunistic infections in presence of a foreign body are called Coagulase negative Staphylococci (CNS). This is an umbrella name covering a number of organisms including Staphylococcus epidermidis, Staphylococcus haemolyticus and many others.

An example of a patient infected with CNS occurred in December 2005. One morning when I was in the process of authorising reports, I came across five consecutive reports from the same patient. They were all samples of tissues taken in theatre. Clinical information given was, 'Infected hip prosthesis –removed. Operation of implant in August 2005'. CNS was isolated from all five specimens. My comment on the report was, 'CNS, a low virulence organism commonly causes joint prosthesis infection which runs an indolent course like this'. The orthopaedic surgeon who removed the prosthesis followed the right procedure by sending five tissues specimens to the laboratory. The more specimens sent, the easier it was to interpret the significance of the organism isolated especially for a skin organism like CNS. According to medical literature, if the organism had been isolated from just one of the five samples, the probability of an infection would have been about 10%. Three out of five raises the probability to more than 90%. The organism was most likely inoculated at the time of the operation and that is why sterile conditions should be maintained during such operations. CNS hides from the host defences by producing 'slime' which also makes it difficult for most antibiotics to get to the organism. Removal of infected implant is the option of choice. There are, however, clinical settings when it is not possible to remove the infected prosthesis. In such circumstances, suppressive therapy with antibiotics is the only option. Going back to our patient, the second implant on the eighty-year-old was free of infection more than year later.

The other common foreign bodies associated with infection with CNS are the vascular access devices. Numerous treatments are given through the blood stream. In order to get secure access to the blood stream, various devices are used. They are usually left in place for a long time allowing skin organisms like CNS to contaminate the device and consequently posing the risk of septicaemia (blood poisoning). Most true CNS septicaemias occur as a result of infected vascular access devices.

Another organism worth a mention is yeast called Candida albicans, which resides in the mouth, throat and gut. It is the causative organism of thrush. As expected, it also causes infections associated with foreign bodies put in those parts of the body. These include voice prostheses inserted when the larynx (voice box) is removed usually for cancer and dentures (causing Candida infected denture stomatitis (infection of the mouth and lips). Once it gets a foothold of a foreign body, Candida is difficult to dislodge. Depending on the material the device is made of, it may have to be replaced with a new one.

The presence of a foreign body makes an individual susceptible to infections caused mainly by organisms of low virulence. With advances in medicine, more foreign parts will be used in our bodies for various reasons. The dangers of infection should not be overlooked. As the causative organisms can also be contaminants, proper interpretation of the results by microbiologists is paramount.

Aged two years I was sitting very close to my mother who is holding my little brother Peter.

Sitting are my two sisters (L to R) Edith and Deborah. My father (standing) was the parish priest in Humura. Photo taken in July 1949.

1956: Sitting front row: (L to R): Me, my sister Phoebe and my brother Peter (passed way in 1991)

Sitting middle row: My parents. My mother, Eseza Kasigala and father Rev. Ananiya Kasigala who was the parish priest at Makonzi parish. Standing at the back: My sister Deborah.

Our first family Radio, model PYE – PE 37–c1951.

1964: I am 17 years old at Kings College Budo.

1970: Two medical students working during the vacation at Kirembe Mines Hospital. I am on the left and Sabuka on the right.

1973: Some of the final year medical students. I am standing 7th from left (with glasses).

1974: I am doing my internship.

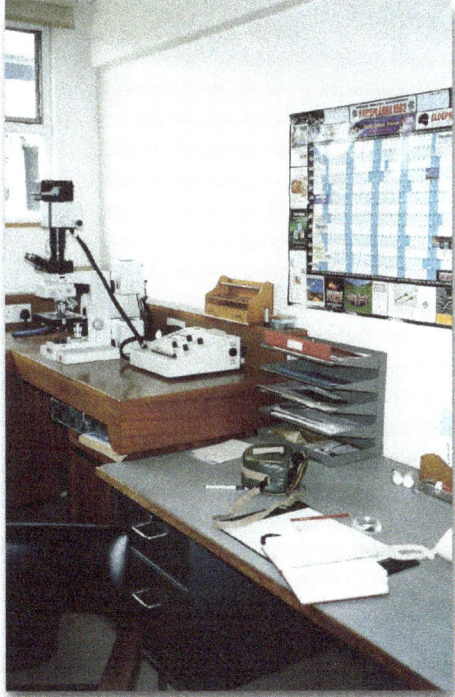

My office in the Canterbury laboratory. I used the microscope in the far corner for almost 30 years.

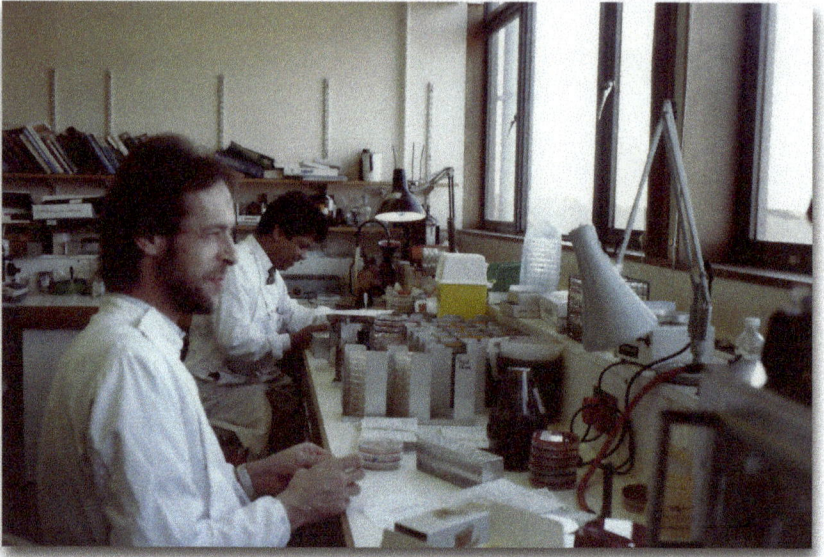

Two senior Biomedical Scientists working side by side in our old microbiology laboratory (vacated in 1994). They are Dave Chetywnd (nearer the camera) and Dave Bissessur. We called them the two Dave's.

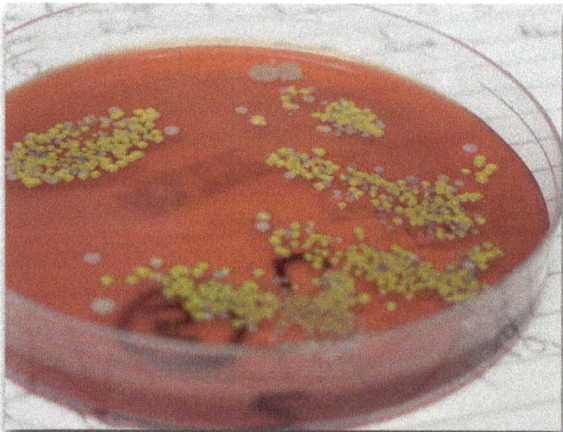

Yellow and grey colonies of bacteria on a plate of blood agar. Biomedical Scientists did tests on these to identify them and find out the most suitable antimicrobial drugs to use to treat the infections the bacteria cause.

1994: Dr Peggy Voysay the Unit manager of Thanet General Hospital was about to cut a ribbon to open the new microbiology laboratory. I had just finished saying a few words.

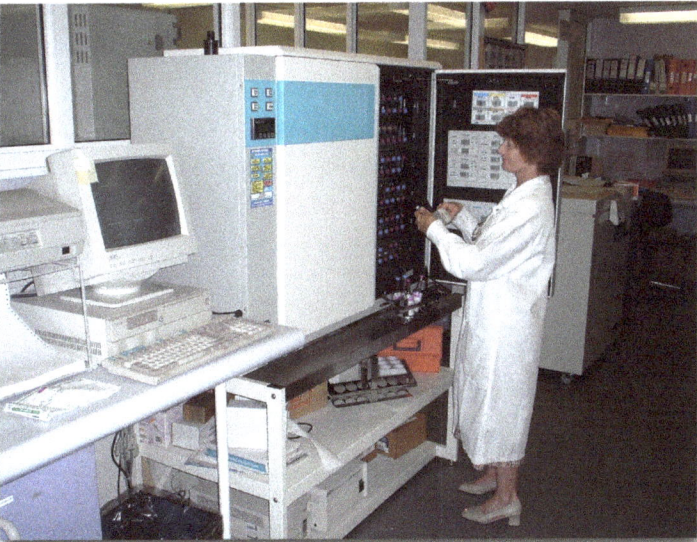

In the new laboratory Carole Thorpe was loading a blood culture machine, which detected septicaemia (blood poisoning) sometimes within hours of the specimens being put in the machine.

18

My Work as Infection Control Doctor

Sometime in 1979 when I was Senior Registrar at Northwick Park, the head of service Dr Philip Sanderson decided to move to Edgware District Hospital. There was a period of a few months when I was in charge of things including infection control. One afternoon, I was thrown in at the deep end when we realised that we had an outbreak of diarrhoea and vomiting on a paediatric ward. I had to call an outbreak meeting and chair it. Those who attended the meeting included Dr David Tyrrell who was a very experienced infectious disease physician and Dr Valman who was head of Paediatrics. These were very knowledgeable people, so my heart was in my mouth as the time of the meeting approached. They made me feel at ease and the meeting went very well. This was the first time I played an important role as an infection control practitioner. I was confident because I had been taught by my mentor Dr Blowers who had just retired. He had taught me to be logical, calm and pay attention to detail. Concrete measures were taken to control the outbreak, which came to an end without any problems.

My next port of call on the infection control matters was at the Middlesex Hospital in central London. There I worked with Dr Robert Edward Mervyn Thompson, an unassuming man of great integrity. He gave me the task of formulating guidelines. This was the beginning of my passion in formulating infection control guidelines. Dr Thompson also talked a lot about the history of the inception of the infection control teams in the UK. He convinced me of the merit of a medical doctor and a nurse forming an ideal infection control team (ICT) – having the right combination of expertise. Later on in my career, I came to a conclusion that in order to have a successful ICT, each member of the team must be dedicated, hardworking and selfless (DHS) assuming that they have the necessary qualifications to do the job.

Two years later, I moved to East Kent to take up the post of consultant microbiologist and infection control doctor – a role I was to play single-handedly for the next seventeen years.

The third of January 1982 was my first day on the job. The first clinician to come to my office to welcome me was the ever helpful and cheerful Dr Michael Goggin, a renal physician who was head of the renal services at the time. He was also the chairman of the infection control committee. He was very supportive but he also had some interesting views on infection control; for example he would not allow anybody including those who had no direct patient contact to enter the renal unit unless they had a negative screening test for hepatitis B. I understood his strict standpoint. Being a blood borne virus, introducing it to a haemodialysis unit would be disastrous. My department did a lot of work for the renal unit including screening both staff and patient for blood borne viruses to prevent spread.

The other large patient group for whom we did a lot work were those on continuous ambulatory peritoneal dialysis (CAPD). Let me explain – kidneys get rid of waste products from the body in the urine they produce. When they fail to do this function, the waste products have to be removed artificially by filtering the blood through a machine outside the body, the process is called haemodialysis or by placing fluid in the abdomen in contact with a membrane called the peritoneum so the waste products from blood go through the membrane to the fluid, which is later removed through a tube to the skin. This process, which is continuous, is called CAPD. Skin organisms can easily contaminate the fluid and cause an infection of the peritoneum otherwise called peritonitis. The majority of these organisms are of low virulence and consequently cause mild infections, but they have to be treated promptly with the right antibiotic to preserve the integrity of the membrane. The microbiology laboratory performed tests to determine the best antibiotics to treat peritonitis.

Every year in the period I was head of service, we held an audit meeting at which I presented information on the types of organisms and the most active antibiotic the renal clinicians could use to treat the infections promptly before the microbiology results were available. Knowing the type of organisms we were dealing with helped us to devise precautions tailor made for a particular organism to prevent further infections. Over the years the number of infections progressively went down.

The audit meetings continued in the 1990s with the new head of the Renal Unit, Dr Paul Stevens. This culminated in a paper, which the two departments published in 2000, on an improved method of early detection of peritonitis in patients of peritoneal dialysis. I look back at this as a triumph for two departments working together to solve a problem. This was a coalition of the willing. Nobody from outside forced us to work together.

For general practitioners, I collected data on causative organisms for urinary infections (*see chapter 12*). The results were sent out annually. Other groups of clinicians did get some survey data but less frequently.

Over the years, East Kent underwent many reorganisations, which impacted on the delivery of services including infection control. For many years, Canterbury and Thanet had one infection control committee. In the mid-1980s two separate units were formed each with its own infection control committee. I was chairman of each committee reporting to two managers. Who said one cannot serve two masters? I formulated the constitutions and terms of reference for the two committees. My committee workload doubled overnight and, you guessed right, without additional financial reward. To make matters worse, I had at the time one infection control nurse covering the two units. I believed then, and still do, that one of the main keys to effective infection prevention and control is the formulation of good guidelines. These were based on:

a) identifying the sources of infection and doing something about them by taking precautions like isolation and use of antibiotics and antiseptics appropriately.
b) blocking modes of transmission – hand hygiene and protective devices like masks and gloves and

c) identifying susceptible individuals or tissues and protecting them appropriately.

All guidelines and talks we gave were based on these simple principles.

At the time of writing this, Ebola is causing major concerns in the world. I will therefore give it as an example in applying the infection control principles. The sources of infection are the people with signs and symptoms as well as objects contaminated with body fluids of the infected people. The sources are dealt with by putting the infected individual into strict isolation and safe disposal of the contaminated objects. Treating an infected person with antiviral drugs will reduce the number of virus particles in the body as well as the duration of illness and therefore the period others can acquire the virus from that source. The susceptible people include health care staff and others who come in very close contact with the infected person. They can be protected by wearing special clothing to cover their eyes, mouth and skin. If a vaccine was available, the susceptible people would be offered one to give them additional protection. There are two main modes of transmission-direct contact and by air. For Ebola, direct contact is the main one. However, if the patient sneezed or coughed, small droplets carrying the virus can be transmitted by air. Protective clothing mentioned above will block this mode of transmission. To prevent the virus-carrying droplets escaping, doors and windows must be closed if simple isolation rooms are being used. I have attempted applying infection control principles to Ebola. All control measures fall in these categories. There are modifications of the control measures depending on the type of infection. Close contacts of a patient with meningococcal meningitis or septicaemia are offered prophylactic antibiotics to protect them. Control measures are also taken to prevent a person's own resident organism invading healthy sterile tissues at the time of certain operations. As a general rule, the amount of effort and cost put on control measures should be proportional to the severity and public health consequences of the infection(s) to be prevented. The extreme example of this rule is that of advising people travelling by public transport in winter to wear a facemask to prevent them catching a common cold in case they sit next to a passenger who is suffering from one. Even if the common cold affects many people, it is a self-limiting mild infection and that is why it is not cost-effective to take such precautions.

In 1989, there was an outbreak of MRSA (Methicillin Resistant Staphylococcus aureus) on the maternity unit at Thanet District General Hospital. We looked for the sources by screening all staff but in vain. A thorough investigation revealed that mattresses were the source of infection. Most mattresses were old and had damaged covers. With the help of a very understanding unit manager Dr Peggy Voysey, all the old mattresses were replaced. That action brought the outbreak to an end.

An effective mattress policy was instituted. After discussions between us and the Medical Devices Directorate of the Department of Health, this became the basis for the national guidelines on the maintenance of mattresses.

As an infection control practitioner, my attitude towards outbreaks was that they were bound to happen, but I had to have the tools to detect them early, to end them early and to learn lessons from them.

Let me throw more light on the organism, Staphylococcus aureus which caused that outbreak. It is a human organism found on our skin, in our noses and other areas. There are two strains of this organism. One sensitive to many relatively cheap antibiotics and therefore cheap to treat is called Methicillin sensitive Staphylococcus aureus (MSSA). The other strain is resistant to many antibiotics and is difficult and expensive to treat. This is called Methicillin resistant Staphylococcus aureus (MRSA). We worry about both strains of Staphylococcus aureus because they cause many infections some of which can be serious and life threatening. If the population of Staphylococcus aureus became predominantly MRSA, the expenditure on the antimicrobial drugs will be very high. This should be the worry for the health care professionals (whose budgets are affected), the taxpayer and the patients who are treated privately. The worry should not be that of the infections being untreatable. MRSA has been flagged to the general public as a dangerous organism and has become synony-mous with dirty hospitals. To make it worse, hospitals have targets to reduce the numbers of MRSA septicaemias (blood poisoning). This is a very narrow and misleading target. MRSA causes many other serious infections, which cause pain and suffering.

The other infection that has made headlines in the popular media is that caused by Clostridium difficile. It is important for the public to have basic relevant information about this organism so that they can work out what is going on when they find themselves or their loved ones in certain situations. There are two strains of this organism- the non-toxigenic strain, which does not produce toxin and the toxigenic strain, which produces a toxin responsible for causing symptoms. The main risk factors for getting the infection include; taking an antibiotic (which reduces the number of normal resident bacteria protecting the gut against potential pathogens from outside), prolonged stay in hospital (more people carry the organism in hospital than outside hospital) and being elderly (8 in 10 cases of C.difficile infection are over 65 years). The symptoms range from mild diarrhoea to life threatening severe diarrhoea and other clinical features. A small number of people carry one or both strains in their gut without symptoms. The other unique feature of this organism is the ability to form spores which are hardy structures adapted to widespread dispersal and survival in unfavourable conditions. A person with Clostridium difficile diarrhoea will disperse millions of spores in the immediate environment.

How can we apply these basic facts to scenarios in which most people are likely to find themselves? Scenario one: You find yourself in hospital next to another patient with diarrhoea and you are worried of catching the much-publicised C.difficile infection. You are right to be concerned because there is a risk, especially when you are elderly and on antibiotics or finished a course; even if the course was as long ago as ten weeks. However, if you are a child the risk is low as this infection is not common in children. The most important point is that this patient should be in isolation far away from you as you may acquire other diarrhoeal infections even if the tests later show that person does not have Clostridium difficile infection. If possible the only practical thing you can do is to make sure you wash your hands frequently especially before a meal. Scenario two: You are in isolation with diarrhoea and C.difficile is suspected. A specimen of stools has been sent to the laboratory. If you have very severe diarrhoea and the risk factors (antibiotics, age and being in hospital for a long time), you should be put on antimicrobial drugs while waiting for the results. The laboratory diagnosis is made with presence of both the organism and its toxin in the stool specimen. The antibiotic therapy will be continued for at least ten days if recurrences are to be avoided. If both organism and toxin are not detected, the cause of the symptoms is unlikely to be C.difficile. For other combinations of results, the laboratory should give clear interpretations and course of action. The ultimate source of confidence for patients in management of C.difficile infection is the efficiency of the infection control team.

Surveillance as mentioned earlier is a very important aspect of infection prevention and control. In 1994, our laboratory acquired a new computer system made by Cerner. It had a good infection control package. I spent a lot of time setting it up. It was labour intensive to run but the dividends of what we got out of it were bountiful. Over the next seven years, it provided very useful surveillance data for the hospital staff as well as general practitioners. It also provided important data to the director of public health. It was not target driven as became the order of the day in later years. We kept a very close eye on certain dangerous pathogens. These included Clostridium difficile (a major cause of infectious diarrhoea), MRSA, multi-resistant Klebsiella (this and other organisms with an umbrella name 'gram negatives' cause a wide range of infections) and Group A Streptococcus (dubbed 'the flesh eating bacteria' by the tabloid press). It was a very useful tool for early detection of outbreaks of these infections as well as those less familiar to the public.

One of the most prevalent gram negative bacteria residing in our gut is an organism called Escherichia coli or E.coli. These normal residents fall into two groups. The majority – three quarters are nice and susceptible to antibiotics. The other quarter is relatively resistant to antibiotics and more pathogenic – they have the propensity to cause infections like urinary tract infections, septicaemias (blood poisoning) among others. When a patient takes an antibiotic say for a sore throat, it will eradicate the organism that causes the sore throat but it will also reduce the number of 'good and protective' E.coli resulting in the 'resistant and more pathogenic' E.coli becoming the predominant organism. The patient will be happy because the sore throat is gone but little will he/she know that there is higher risk of having an infection caused by the resistant E.coli. This information should be made available to patients in case they are interested.

Whether reasons for use of antibiotics are justified or not, there is pressure on resident organisms to become resistant (a natural response to survive). This resistance can spread to other organisms by numerous mechanisms. These resistant strains can also be passed on to other people by contact. We can reduce the increase in resistance and spread by eliminating the unjustified use of antibiotics as well as good hand hygiene. As long as antibiotics are used, the risk of resistance will remain.

Every Thursday afternoon, I filled in my weekly returns for the communicable disease report (CDR) for the Margate laboratory and I did the same thing for the Canterbury laboratory on Fridays. The Communicable Diseases Surveillance Centre Colindale near London compiled a weekly report based on the returns collected from all laboratories in England and Wales. The CDR consisted of pathogens of interest.

In 1991, one winter Thursday afternoon, I was filling in one of these returns when I noticed that the numbers of a parasite called Cryptosporidium had dramatically gone up over that of the previous week. I quickly looked up the data for the previous three weeks. The numbers had been steadily going up. Cryptosporidium is a parasite, which causes diarrhoea. It is normally found in the gut of animals. I scrutinised the data and found that all the cases were coming from a small area around the towns of Broadstairs, Margate and Ramsgate. To cut a long story short, we found out that the source was surface water from River Stour at a place called Plutts Gutter, which had been used to supplement borehole water after a long drought. The chlorine resistant parasite had survived the treatment process. Stopping the use of surface water brought the outbreak to an end. Interestingly, one hundred and forty years earlier, a famous physician by the name of John Snow working in London had ended the notorious water borne cholera outbreak by removing a handle from a water pump. In both instances, it was the meticulous collection and analysis of data that solved the problem. Over the years, I picked up many outbreaks by careful scrutiny of data. In the later years of my career, I noticed that there was a tendency among infection control practitioners to replace the collection and meticulous scrutiny of data with holding numerous meetings to discuss scanty inadequate data. It is my view that this is not a good trend.

Surveillance, took many forms. Sometimes, it involved detailed clinical work on my part. An example of this, was working out the incidence (the number of cases in defined period) of ventilator-associated pneumonia in one of our intensive therapy units (ITU). If breathing is interrupted deliberately or by disease, a machine called a ventilator is used to help the affected individual to continue breathing. The process of using a ventilator disrupts the host defences against respiratory infections including pneumonia. This type of pneumonia is called ventilator-associated pneumonia (VAP) that can be very severe and life-threatening. In 2005 I set out to investigate the magnitude of this problem. First, I had to define VAP by determining the clinical features of VAP. These included chest X-ray changes, abnormal blood gases (indicating that the lungs were malfunctioning) and fever among others. With the help of the intesivists and other clinical staff, I was able to work out the incidence of VAP in the Margate ITU. This formed the baseline to gauge future trends. If a patient developed VAP, this is the kind information relatives and friends should get from the doctor looking after that patient. They would like to know how common the condition is and the likely outcome. Someone in the organisation has to work hard to get this local information.

At that time the infection control doctor with the help of the infection control nurses, was a jack-of-all-trades and a reasonable master of some of them. This included laundry, kitchens, sterilisers, operating theatres, and cleanliness of walls, quality of drinking water and others. Some of these were beyond our direct control but because they had infection control implications, we had to have an overview of all of them. I remember keeping the issue of sorting out taps of drinking water for more than a year on the agenda of the infection control committee. The works department people took a long time to do the job despite numerous reminders from me.

When I set up the two infection control committees, one of the tasks I had to perform was to decide on the composition of the committees. The guiding principle I used was that, to be a member of the committee, one had to either represent a group or department or had some relevant expertise. If it was a one-off service to the committee, that individual could be co-opted or be given a special invitation for one agenda item. This approach saved a lot of valuable time for all concerned.

As chairman of the committee I encouraged every member of the committee to make a contribution. This was partly done by drawing up a good varied agenda giving members plenty of time to come up with agenda items. I tried to avoid mistakes made by other committees I had served on where members were excluded from giving meaningful contributions

In 2000, the Public Health Laboratory Service (PHLS) was awarded the responsibility of providing the microbiology and infection control service to East Kent. I relinquished my duties as the infection control doctor for Canterbury and Thanet. Although, I was still a member of the team, the approach to infection control was very different. We moved into the world of targets. The first asset to go was the Cerner computer system, which as I mentioned before, had a good infection control package. Despite that and other changes, I embarked on new challenges.

With the help of a very enthusiastic infection control nurse called Martin Cutter, I carried out a little experiment on the effect of visible wall signs on the use of hand wash detergent on one ward. Large signs indicated where the wash basins were located and instructions to wash hands before and after any procedure involving direct patient care as well as before and after entering the ward were placed prominently on the walls. The consumption of hand washing detergent was measured over a defined period before and after putting up the signs. The difference was astounding – a massive 175 % rise in the use of the detergent. We reported this in a letter to the editor of the Journal of Hospital Infection in 2001. It was entitled '"Road signs" approach to hand hygiene'. Coincidentally, a few months later, there was a national campaign on hand hygiene as a very important tool in infection prevention and control. It is pleasing to know that hand hygiene rubs are widely used in many countries all over the world, but more needs to be done.

I still had some memorable incidents. One of these took place in December 2004 when there was an outbreak of Norovirus gastroenteritis at Queen Elizabeth the Queen Mother Hospital (formerly called Thanet District General Hospital). It affected more than 150 patients and 40 staff over a period of several weeks.

The main symptom of this viral infection is vomiting. The virus is highly infectious. Control measures include early diagnosis, isolating the affected patients and closing wards to new admissions if it is an outbreak. As the infection control lead, at that hospital, I tried to introduce a form for rapid data collection by the ward staff. The data included the number of new patients with symptoms as well as those having symptoms again after getting better, staff affected and the number of empty beds on the ward. The form also had a summary of the main clinical features of this infection to make it easy for staff to make the diagnosis. This information would be collected by staff who knew the patients very well. This proposal was turned down by the other members of the infection control team. It was decided that it was the members of the infection control team who would go to the ward and make assessments of the patients.

This approach was plausible at the time because there were many infection control practitioners. This old problem of people justifying their jobs by trying to do other peoples' jobs happens in other organisations. There is also an issue of trust or lack of it, that a group of professional people cannot be trusted to do their job. It was reported at another hospital that some members of the infection control doing this practice of interviewing patients themselves went down with Norovirus – a very unfortunate strategic position as it resulted into an acute shortage of infection control practitioners whose jobs are so specialised that other staff cannot be deployed to cover. Infection control is everybody's responsibility. All healthcare staff should be trained to perform their duties all the time including times of outbreaks. When I was infection control doctor that was the only option I had, as the infection team was very small.

I would not have done my work as infection control doctor without the help and support of a dedicated infection control team. At various times during my tenure, (from 1982 to 2000), the team included Margaret Leonard, Lucy Brown, Linda Dempster, Sue Roberts and Martin Cutter.

As time went on I decided to concentrate more on anti-microbial guidelines, which were an integral part of infection prevention and control. I became chairman of the Antibiotic Stewardship Group, a job I did from 2007 to 2011.

I will end this chapter by mentioning a recent conversation I had with a group of close friends. It was about patient choice in connection with hospital infections. Up to that moment, they were worried about what they had read in the popular press-MRSA, Clostridium difficile, Group A Streptococcus (flesh-eating bacteria), babies dying of blood poisoning and a few others. I pointed out that most hospitals were keeping a close eye on these infections and were achieving the set targets. I told them that there were many other hospital-acquired infections, some of which would be caused by one's own organisms. The informed choice should be based on the efficiency of the infection control team (ICT), headed by the infection control doctor. After the passage of the Health and Social care Act of 2008, the director of infection prevention (DIPC) replaced the ICD as the leader of the team. The confidence you put in the DIPC should be based on his/her track record – control of outbreaks, surveillance of all infections rather than just MRSA bacteraemia and Clostridium difficile. I would be wary of a DIPC who spends huge amount of resources on MRSA control to meet the targets at the expense of other infections, which can also cause fatalities. I would also have concerns when I read about a DIPC whose audience consists of mainly senior managers and those who set the targets. Hospital websites should make their DIPC's credentials available to the public. This information should include proof of their sound knowledge on a wide range of pathogens, epidemiology and antimicrobial drugs as well as being good teachers able to pass on knowledge to the rest of the team. It would be desirable to have information on the appointment process for these very important people responsible for preventing and controlling infections. All this would give potential patients like my friends confidence in the system especially in cases of emergencies when they may not have a choice on which hospital they are taken to. When the opportunities arise, choice should be based on the exhibited quality of the DIPC and not so much on the notes on MRSA and Clostridium difficile posted on hospital websites. Confidence should be based on the fact that a good DIPC will deal with all eventualities of health care associated infections.

19

Descriptive Diagnosis Becomes my Pet Subject

In my early years, whenever I had a glass of milk, I developed abdominal pain, distention and felt generally very unwell. It was years later when I became a doctor that I made a diagnosis of lactose intolerance. Lactase is an enzyme which helps to digest lactose; a sugar in milk. I had stopped drinking milk and always took my coffee or tea black. I made a similar diagnosis for my mother who had never taken milk. She had always said that she did not like the smell of milk. She however, had symptoms similar to mine when she ate bread, which she loved. When I realised that milk was used in making bread that clinched the diagnosis for her. Later on I would send her lactase tablets so that she could still enjoy her bread without the unpleasant symptoms. A few years ago, most supermarkets started selling lactose free milk, so now I too can enjoy a bowl of cereal with milk – very nice.

Most people are familiar with the word diagnosis in connection with disease. It is usually the answer to the question, 'What is wrong with me doc?' As far as infection is concerned, terms like 'chest infection', 'measles' and 'Flu' are quite familiar.

One of my main responsibilities as a consultant microbiologist was formulating antimicrobial guidelines for hospitals as well as general practitioners (*see chapter 10*). The guidelines usually consisted of a list of infections and their treatments. As time went on, I realised that the terms like 'pneumonia' were too general, so I decided to 'fine tune' them by going into more details of the way I selected antibiotics. The selection of an antibiotic for a particular infection depends on many factors relating to the patient (host), the causative organism and the antibiotic itself. The host factors include age, pregnancy and susceptibility to infection among many others. The susceptibility to infection is determined by the integrity of host defences.

I would like to go into more details of this as it is the key to understanding term 'susceptibility to infection'. The host defences are there to defend against organisms from outside the body as well the ones resident inside. These defences are divided into two major groups – general and local. The general defences include white blood cells in form of neutrophils and lymphocytes as well as other substances. The local factors refer to individual systems of the body, particularly those colonised with resident micro-organisms. These include the gastrointestinal tract or the gut, the respiratory tract, the urinary tract (concerned with formation and passing of urine), genital tract (female and male) and skin. The latter is a very important host defence as it covers a large part of the body. The local defences also produce substances like anti-bodies and have local cells specialised to prevent the invasion into deeper tissues by the resident organisms as well as the occasional foreign organisms.

The organism factors include virulence. Very virulent organisms can cause very severe infections, which need prompt treatment. The elimination of the causative organism depends on the integrity of the host defences and the antibiotic. If the host defences are impaired or reduced, the elimination will depend on the antibiotic alone. That antibiotic should be potent enough to do the job. It should be remembered that in the pre-antibiotic era, the human race depended on the host defences to fight infections but of course many people perished. The doctors should know the likely causative organisms in order to give the right treatment. It was my job as a microbiologist to give the clinicians that information.

The descriptive diagnosis covers all three groups of factors. It also gives information on the duration of the infection, where the infection was acquired (indicating the types of causative organisms) and sometimes prognosis. An example of such diagnosis will be:

Severe (indicator of prognosis) community acquired Pneumococcal (the causative organism causing an infection with the onset in the community) pneumonia (infection of lungs) in an elderly man (waning general host defences) with neutropenia (devoid of neutrophils which kill bacteria). Most of the words or phrases in that example have treatment implications. Mentioning the site of infection – in this example lungs – is very important because some antibiotics do not reach the site in high enough concentrations to kill the causative organism. Generally, the more relevant descriptive terms used, the better the refinement and the more likely the doctor will choose the right antibiotic.

Use of word 'severe' can have major connotations on the management of infection. According to some experts, each hour of delay of effective treatment (the delay includes the time patient is on the wrong antibiotic) from the onset of hypotension (low blood pressure – which can be a sign of severe infection), carries an eight percent reduction in survival. In such cases, speed of action with the right antibiotic is of essence and all the components of the descriptive diagnosis must be attended to. Criteria for severity have been produced for some infections. For example a five point score based on confusion, urea (a waste product from the breakdown of proteins), respiratory rate, blood pressure and age of over 65 – with an acronym of CURB-65 is used to assess the severity of community acquired pneumonia.

In a nutshell, descriptive diagnosis is a formal statement that includes relevant words or phrases with treatment and management implications. In cases of infections, descriptive diagnosis should include a good explanation to the patient why an antibiotic is indicated or not.

If a patient had a urinary tract infection with an obstruction to the flow of urine, the descriptive diagnosis could be 'Complicated urinary tract infection' indicating that antibiotics alone would not cure that infection unless the obstruction is removed and the flow of urine, which is the main host defence of the urinary tract, is restored.

Another example is a person with heart failure and pneumonia. Fluid accumulates in the lungs of people with heart failure.

The elimination of organisms from wet lungs is difficult. For that patient, heart failure should be mentioned in the descriptive diagnosis of pneumonia.

I encouraged my clinical colleagues to use descriptive diagnosis making it easy for them to choose the right antibiotic rationally. This also empowers patients to know the exact nature of their infections so that when they ask the question, 'what is wrong with me doc?' the answer should be a descriptive diagnosis indicating all the important aspects of managing the infection.

Some clinicians are scared of being wrong, the consequences of which may lead to litigation. My approach to this problem has been the use of the phrase 'provisional diagnosis' and stating the clinical evidence; including history. If a previously healthy young person presents to his doctor with a common cold, the doctor will state that the provisional diagnosis is a viral upper respiratory tract infection in previously healthy young man. He can only write this after taking history and performing a physical examination. He can write in his notes and tell him that an antibiotic is not necessary at this point but may be required if the diagnosis changed. This process can save a lot of money spent on unnecessary antibiotics for such patients. However, if another young man presented with the same symptoms but the provisional diagnosis was a viral upper respiratory tract infection with neutropenia (reduced functional white cells); the doctor may prescribe an antibiotic because this infection could suddenly become complicated as this particular patient has defective host defences. Regular review of patients especially inpatients is essential because new symptoms and signs may appear sometimes making it necessary to change the diagnosis dramatically or adding more descriptive terms in the original diagnosis; both requiring change of therapy.

The courses different infections take vary. There are those that last a short period (acute) and others that run a prolonged course to become chronic. The terms acute and chronic are used in the descriptive diagnosis. They are also used in the interpretation of laboratory tests. A negative laboratory test for an infection and the test of time can enable a microbiologist to conclude that the suspected infection is unlikely. For example if the laboratory test for flu is negative in an individual who has had flu-like symptoms for months (flu symptoms last at most two weeks), the diagnosis of flu is very unlikely. This has therapeutic implications and demonstrates the importance of proper history taking in the management of infections. Ideally, with such history that test should not be performed. One of the responsibilities of a microbiologist is to cut costs by not doing unnecessary tests.

The tool of descriptive diagnosis can also be used in determining and monitoring the duration of therapy, which ranges from a single dose to many weeks. Prolonged unnecessary antibiotic therapy is a waste of resources and leads to the emergence of resistance in resident organisms, which can cause infections in that individual and others in contact with him/her. On the other hand, stopping too early carries the risks of relapses and development of resistance in the causative organism. Therefore, getting the duration right is very important and can only be achieved by having a well-defined diagnosis.

All this information should be revealed to the patient and other health care staff who may review or take over the care of the patient. Patients are increasingly becoming aware of the benefits and bad effects of antibiotics. It is important to inform them of the way doctors make decisions on the use of this group of drugs.

Descriptive diagnosis will become more precise as we learn more about the genetic determinants for susceptibility to infection. The successful completion of the Human Genome Project in 2003 was a very important landmark. At last, the human genome had been unravelled. One hopes that in future it will be possible to look at an individual's genetic make-up and be able to predict the likely descriptive diagnosis of an infection caused by a particular organism. This will have prevention and treatment implications. Prevention measures like vaccination will probably be considered for such individuals and treatment will be started early when they present with features suggestive of a particular infection. The genetic determinants are responsible for the way the body responds to infection. In some individuals, the response to infection causes considerable damage to the body. If clinical markers of the damage can be identified, they should be part of the descriptive diagnosis and therefore part of the treatment. Leprosy, a rare disease in most countries, is an example of the varying degree a body responds to Mycobacterium leprae, its causative organism. At one extreme is tuberculosis leprosy to which the body reacts strongly and contains the organism but damages the nerves in the process. At the other extreme, is lepromatuous leprosy, to which the body hardly responds, allowing the organisms to run amok resulting into large numbers of them in the body. I came across such a patient at Northwick Park Hospital. His specimens were teaming with organisms.

Descriptive diagnosis of infections has implications on the formulation of antimicrobial guidelines and coding of infections for the purpose of data collection. Dare I suggest that the term can also be used in other branches of medicine as well as social and economic conditions? In all instances, proper and accurate descriptive terms should be used when effective remedies are being considered.

20

Our Beloved NHS: The Descriptive Diagnosis and Remedy

It was a fine warm day in 1996, I was one of the many people standing in line patiently waiting to greet Prince Charles who had come to open a new extension of the Queen Elizabeth the Queen Mother Hospital at Margate. He eventually reached our group. He exchanged a few words with those who were in the line in front of us and off he went to talk to the next group. That was the closest I had ever been to him. As I walked back to my office through the corridors of this brand new part of the hospital, I said to myself, 'This is the NHS at its best'. Then my mind went back to the black and white photograph I had seen in a newspaper of Aeurin Bevan who launched the NHS in 1948. He would be proud of the size it had become not to mention the millions of people that had been treated in its institutions free at the point of delivery and use. Like any good family, it had taken care of all its members well irrespective of gender, age, social status or income.

Like most families, sometimes things do not go according to plan. As a person who had worked for the NHS for twenty years, I noticed some aspects of the organisation had gone astray. After yet another configuration of the NHS or the publication of yet another report of an outbreak of deaths of babies together with the inevitable numerous recommendations, my casual comment to close colleagues and friends was always, 'It is the system which is malfunctioning. Until it is fixed, these incidents will continue to occur'. The people I was talking to would shrug their shoulders and life would continue as before.

In 1997, the then new Secretary of State for Health, Frank Dobson was looking for new ideas of how to improve the health service, so he invited proposals from the public and health care staff. As this was a new government, I decided to put pen to paper. My ideas were quite radical and I thought they would address the fundamental faults in acute hospitals on roles played by the key people namely the Chief Executive, Clinical Directors, Consultants and Clinical services managers. In the last chapter, I stressed the importance of making an accurate descriptive diagnosis in the treatment of infections. That approach applies to other areas of life. The diagnosis here was unsuitable people being in senior management posts promoting their personal interests. To be fair to them, successive governments have tried to tackle this problem with varying degree of success.

The fundamental point of my proposal was that people should be employed to do a job they are qualified to do and in a hospital that job would involve direct patient care most of the time. In my proposal, the key people would be the Medical Director (who would be elected by Consultants or heads of service), Director of Nursing (who would be elected by senior nurses of departments) and heads of clinical services. All these people would form the clinical board, which would be chaired by the Medical Director who would still do some sessions of direct patient care. The clinical board would appoint other members of the board namely, the hospital administrator (in charge of the 'hotel' activities), the Director of Finance and Director of Human Resources. The election of the key people would create confidence among the majority of the hard working staff. This was mainly about accountability and confidence.

At the District Health Authority level (which was there at the time and was closely linked to the acute units), I suggested that the board should consist of three key people – the District Medical Officer, the consultant in communicable disease control and the treasurer.

I posted the proposal and waited for a response in vain. This was not surprising as mine was one of thousands of proposals the secretary of state received but I was satisfied that I had expressed my views.

In late 1997, a review of the cervical screening programme at Kent and Canterbury hospital was published. Once again comments were invited by the secretary of state. Although this was a specific problem of mistakes made in the screening of cervical cancer at that hospital, the fundamental faults were similar to the ones I pointed out before. So in early November, I sent a similar proposal to the then Minister of State for Health Baroness Jay and once again nothing happened. I was not surprised because busy ministers get many such letters and it is unrealistic to expect changes to take place as a result of comments like mine.

Fast forward to November 2010 another reorganisation was under way. This time, it was being carried out by the coalition government of the Conservative party and the Liberal Democrats. The new government was looking for suggestions. I was about to retire but I felt duty bound to send some suggestions from my experience of more than thirty years in the NHS. The structures were slightly different but the fundamentals problems were still there. This time the descriptive diagnosis was that of;

1) A highly bureaucratic system with layers of management creating heavy committee workload diverting senior staff away from direct patient care.
2) Well remunerated management jobs enticing talented clinical staff to do them leading to a reduction in the time they spend on direct patient care.
3) Target driven practice reducing time clinician have for proper care of patients.
4) Amalgamation of departments for the benefit of senior managers without any demonstrable benefit to patients.
5) The wrong people in senior management posts perpetuating policies and practices designed to protect their jobs.
6) Weakened management at departmental level

However, I knew of several heads of departments who were very good at their jobs and provided excellent service to their patients but could have done an even better job if they worked with people with similar qualities. The common pathway for many of them was to move to more senior managerial posts within the hospital or to outside organisations like the royal colleges. That was the only way most talented people could improve their chances of getting higher merit awards. This was good for them but not necessarily good for their departments and the long-term benefit for their patients. There were bound to be minor variations of the descriptive diagnosis as we moved from one hospital to another, but the underlying problems were much the same. Like infections, the problems can also move from acute to chronic and if they are left to fester, treatment can be costly. Having made the diagnosis of the ailment of the NHS, the next step was to find a remedy. The main temptation is to treat the symptoms, which include waiting times and disasters as they are reported in the media.

The descriptive diagnosis of the NHS is thus, a bureaucratic (non-medical as well as medical), target-driven organisation with reduced direct patient care and weakened management at departmental level. Some components of the descriptive diagnosis need more urgent treatment than others. I took the basic functional unit of the hospital to be the department as stipulated below. Once that was sorted out, the rest would fall into place. That was why I concentrated on the heads of department – their qualifications and how they were appointed.

The core feature of the remedy in my proposal was to strengthen individual clinical departments by appointing high quality heads of these departments. The twenty or so departments included Accident and Emergency, Anaesthetics, Cellular pathology (with Immunology as a sub-department in non-tertiary centres), Children's Health, Clinical Biochemistry (liaising with General Medicine to run lipid clinics), General Medicine (with deputy heads for Dermatology, Gastroenterology, Neurology and Rheumatology), General Surgery (with deputy head for Plastic surgery), Health Care for Older People, Haematology (with deputy head for Haemophilia), Immunology (in tertiary centres) Maxillofacial Surgery, ENT (Ear, Nose and Throat), Mental Health, Microbiology (Deputy head for Virology – depending on local expertise and Director of Infection Prevention and Control), Ophthalmology, Radiology, Renal Medicine, Trauma and Orthopaedics (with deputy head for physiotherapy), Urology, Vascular Surgery, Women's Health and Pharmacy. Each clinical department should be allocated wards. This would make infection control and antibiotic prescribing easier to monitor. Each department will be a complete functional unit with options to form associations with other departments within or outside the Trust. These would be coalitions of the willing and not imposed from outside. Depending on the type of department, each would have a wide range of staff – medical, nursing, technicians, porters and cleaners. Each department would be responsible for training, formulation of guidelines as well as dealing with health and safety issues.

To manage all this would require a special professional person – the Executive Head of Department. The recruitment of such a person was the key feature of the proposal. I listed some essential qualities including:

1) Intelligence (including emotional intelligence) – psychometric tests may help in the assessment if deemed necessary.
2) Sound knowledge of their subject.
3) Leadership and strategic planning.
4) Ability to translate medical literature into effective therapy.
5) Ability to carry out research.
6) Ability to recognise talent and people with good ideas.
7) Head of service should be personable but not become personal with his or her staff.

These are not theoretical qualities as I have come across heads of departments lacking some of these qualities to the detriment of their departments and damage to patient care. Take emotional intelligence as an example – the right way of interacting with people is crucial in running a successful department. The head should have the ability to put staff at ease. Unrealistic expectations from staff can cause stress for the head as well as staff.

The selection of the interview panel would be crucial. Over the years, heads of service have been appointed in a dysfunctional system. It is risky and unhelpful to appoint a person to this important position because he/she happened to be working in the department at the time. The system needs a robust overhaul.

Therefore, if necessary, specialist from abroad or outside the system should be invited to be members of the interviewing panels. After all this is what is done in singing competitions in which competitors are put through their paces to find the very best. Surely our health needs even more rigorous tests. The main criteria should not be based on the best person to work with senior managers. It is vital that the appointee carries the confidence of the consultant and other senior staff in that department. I heard through the grapevine that every capable highly professional person was not appointed to a senior management post because that individual did not fit the 'boardroom' image. In order to attract good candidates, the remuneration of the post of head of service should be very good, but bearing in mind that being head of service gives the post holder an opportunity to excel and earn excellence awards. Clinical heads of departments would be responsible for keeping within their budgets to avoid periods of 'lean' years alternating with years of 'plenty'. The tenure for the head of department should be determined by the clinical board. A good head of service should not allow personal ambitions to hinder recruiting other good people to the department. Good doctors know their limitations and know when to seek advice or refer patients. If a specialist is really good, he would not seek or try to persuade managers to close other units to make his or her departments larger. I call this 'empire building' and in my experience has ulterior motives. Patients will look for such specialist because of the work they have done to give them a good reputation. Trainee doctors who work with such good specialist will go to other hospitals and spread the good practices. Good units cannot be artificially created by managers or politicians based on advice given by doctors looking after their own interests. Good departments can only grow organically and take a long time to build and nurture. There are some professions in which duration of practice and experience turns the possessor into an accomplished professional. Medicine is one of these professions. At the moment, there is an increasing tendency for some doctors to get lured away into management without spending enough time practicing what they were qualified to do. This eventually lowers standards of patient care.

Heads of department would form the Clinical Management Board, which would meet quarterly. This may sound very prescriptive but I know for sure it would save a lot of time currently spent by senior consultants on committee work (*see chapter 11*). As most policies would be produced at department level, the Board would deal with general matters such as clinical governance, audits, research and financial matters. The Board would be chaired by the Medical Director, who would be elected by heads of service from the board members. The Medical director would have gone through the rigor of the interview for head of service. This would give credibility and confidence to the post holder. He/she should be paid well to recognise these qualities. As all the departments will be managed efficiently, the Medical Director can still be the head of his/her own department with support from within the department. At the end of the tenure of say three years, he/she can continue with normal duties without much disruption to the patient care. Deputy medical directors should also be appointed to chair subcommittees on research, audit and clinical governance. The Medical Director should be the link between the Clinical Board and non-medical department/personnel, who would include the Hospital Manager who would deal with the legal matters and 'hotel' activities of the hospital, the Finance department and Human resources.

There is also the issue of responsibility when things go wrong. In this proposal the lines of responsibility are clearly defined. Take a scenario of a fifty-year-old man with infectious pneumonia lying for many hours in the accident and emergency department waiting for a bed on a medical ward. The heads of the two departments (A&E and General Medicine) are responsible for his care. The other component of his management is the prevention of the spread of infection from him to other people. The two heads or their teams should get advice from the infection control team who are responsible for formulating guidelines for dealing with such infectious patients. In this scenario, three heads of service are responsible for his care. If there are financial or strategic problems which prevent them carrying out their work efficiently, these can be discussed by the whole Clinical Management Board consisting of other heads of department who as mentioned above were appointed for their exceptional abilities to solve problems. I believe that there is the right and wrong way of tackling problems. The carefully selected heads of departments should be right most of the time.

Good and well-managed departments are fertile soil for research and clinical audit opportunities. Such departments will also be sources of high calibre potential employees of other NHS and private hospitals as well as other organisations like the World Health Organisation (WHO).

I put some of these points in a proposal to the Minister of Health but this time, I decided to go through my Member of Parliament, Mr Julian Brazier. I met him in his surgery. He was very patient to listen to what I had to say and agreed to take my proposal to the minister concerned. After just a few days, I was delighted to get a response through my MP from Mr Simon Burns the then Minister responsible for NHS performance. He thanked me for my suggestions and made reference to the White Paper, 'Equity and excellence: Liberating the NHS' and the intention of the government to cut the NHS management costs by forty-five percent. He also referred me to the documents of what was being done. I was happy that I had done my duty to point out what was happening in the NHS. Since then I have put more 'meat' on the proposal as presented here.

It is now more than three years since I got that response. A few more outbreaks have occurred and inquires have been set up. Governments of all persuasions do their best to improve patient care within the constraints of the prevailing economic climate. What I was proposing was not to increase expenditure. On the contrary, it was going to save money. This principle of recruiting the right people applies in other spheres of national and international activities. Once the right head has been appointed, the right people are bound to be appointed in that department. This will eventually liberate the NHS from constant political interference. I feel that health should not be treated as a 'political football'. I really believe that the roles and quality of heads of the above mentioned departments should be underpinned by legislation. In the initial stages of implementation, the current heads of service can become acting heads until the proper selection process has taken place.

I also believe that anybody, rich or poor, influential or ordinary needs a good clinical service. That is why this proposal should be of interest to everybody. Many doctors have done or are doing well in the current system as evidenced by the number of excellence awards given out annually. Their response to changes in the status quo is likely to be, 'If it isn't broken, do not fix it'. 'After all,' they would argue, 'There are thousands of patients who get an excellent service and are grateful for it'.

On the other side of the coin, there are many frustrated health care professionals who suffer from low morale despite the fact that they too work very hard. There are also many patients who do not get the service they deserve. These proposals would lead to a 'win win' situation for all – NHS workers and patients as well as private practitioners and patients.

This proposed structure is likely to make sense to patients. When a patient with a complicated illness goes to his or her GP, the real choice for the patient and the GP should be to select the best specialist – ophthalmologist (if it is an eye problem), cardiologist (if it is a heart problem) and so on. The choice should be based on the reputation of the specialist. It is that specialist who should publish his or her work including death rates, complications and other relevant data so that the GP and the patient can make an informed choice. Medical conditions have different complications. These include bleeding, clot formation, infection and many others. When complications arise, the affected patient needs reassurance that the attending doctor is competent to deal with them. At this stage, confidence is crucial as it contributes a lot to the patient's general wellbeing, which may affect outcome. All this gives the patients and their general practitioners real and meaningful choices at the beginning of the process.

The other way patients make choices is by word of mouth. When friends and relatives sought my opinion on choice, the question was always, 'Which doctor do you recommend?' Good doctors and other health care professionals make good departments, which in turn make good hospitals. This reminded me of that proverb – 'fine feathers make fine birds'. The quality of doctors has a knock on effect on private hospitals as many NHS specialists also work in private hospitals. The message usually sent to the public is the size of the Trust and equating this to quality.

The bottom line is that when the right doctor is in charge, all things are likely to make sense to the patient – the diagnosis and treatment. I get the same experience with plumbers and electricians when they come to my house to do various jobs. The good ones make sense when they explain things to me.

Activities like revalidation (the process by which the General Medical Council will confirm the continuation of a doctor's licence to practice in the UK) and publishing of death rates by individual doctors will have a limited impact on the overall quality of care unless the doctors work in departments managed by effective heads of service. Take a case of a person going for an operation. The outcome is influenced by the anaesthetics given (controlled by anaesthetist), the surgical technique (wholly controlled by the surgeon), theatre discipline (team effort), operating room air standards (team effort) and post operation care (team effort). That is why an individual surgeon can only excel when she /he is working in good department headed by a person who understands and has the authority to control all those factors.

Simplifying the management structure by abolishing the Directorates would be the first step in reforming the malfunctioning structure. In my own field of pathology, the directorate consisted of four departments namely haematology, clinical chemistry, histopathology and microbiology. The practice was to appoint a clinical director from the consultant staff in the four departments. That individual would have little or no knowledge of the other three departments. It gets worse – a proposal was made and later implemented to put pathology and radiology (dealing with imaging) under one management structure. Under this proposal, it was possible for a microbiologist like me to be the manager of that huge structure and the main attraction to that job was better remuneration. The fact of the matter is that I would not be qualified to do that job which would involve managing radiology and the other three departments of pathology. Even a course in management would not give the qualification to do that job. The course may make me a better manager for microbiology. Reducing bureaucracy should apply to both medical and non-medical staff.

'I am a poacher turned gamekeeper,' was the response of a friend and colleague of mine to my congratulating him on his appointment to a very senior management position. Before that he had been very critical of many management decisions. Many people I knew were of the attitude – 'It is my turn to earn more money' when they sought senior management positions. Most of them spent a lot of time at meetings with senior non-medical managers. I attended some of these meeting and found the majority to be clearly otiose (*see chapter 11*).

For decades from 1970s onwards, the clinical departments were grouped into Divisions. The rule in most cases for selecting the heads of departments and chairs of divisions was 'Buggins turn' (awarding promotion by rotation rather than merit). Things did not really improve when Directorates replaced Divisions.

The issue of how the NHS is funded has to be settled by a proper national debate. Many people have a noble intention of putting more funds into the NHS. They talk about more doctors, more nurses among others. The simple analogy I use on this matter is that of a leaking bucket. Will anyone ever hope to fill the bucket by pouring in more water? The first logical step is to repair the hole. In a dysfunctional organisation, money is likely to be wasted; staff will leave because of stress and low morale.

As far as the NHS and private hospitals are concerned and having worked in both for a long time, it is my view that they can have a mutually beneficial co-existence.

21

The Changing Faces of Interviews Over the Years

When I first became a consultant microbiologist and head of service in 1982, the whole process of recruiting staff to the department was a local affair. I knew my department inside out, including the skill mix and personalities of my staff. I was involved in the whole process for all staff ranging from the head of biomedical scientist to the laboratory assistant. The gist of the exercise was to get the right person for the job. I took this task very seriously because selecting the right people is one of the pivotal activities for any successful organisation. We paid attention to detail to all the phases of the process; namely the job description, advertising, shortlisting, choice of the interview panel and the interview itself. To varying degrees, most senior members of staff were involved in the process, for example, when a candidate was taken around the department before the interview, staff had the opportunity to talk to the candidate and get the first impressions of the person.

Setting scenarios for candidates was a favourite of mine. This gave me the confidence that the person could do the job the following day. This included practical questions, for example, reading out names of organisms in case of a bench clerk whose job involved giving microbiology results over the telephone. This identified people who would never be able to do certain tasks however much they were trained.

Assessing an individual's character is a challenge. Before modern techniques were available, we had to depend on observation and asking the right questions. For example, there was this young man who leaned forward very close to the face to the member of the panel asking the question. He was really invading the space of the interviewer. We had to know something about body language as an important form of communication. Another example was that of a girl who had this nervous laugh, which was so infectious that the panel also joined in the laughter!

We as interviewers had to have some knowledge of the personality types of the people especially the senior members of staff we already had in the departments. We had introverts, extroverts, intuitive types, judging, feeling types among others. This had to be born in mind as we interviewed new people to create diversity but avoid destructive clashes of personalities.

Over the years I interviewed many high flyers. I was always wary of high flyers whose story was just about themselves and not doing things for the benefit of the whole department. Such people turn out to be selfish leaders who only think of 'ME'. Experience has shown that they do well for themselves but their departments and those who work with them may suffer.

The emphasis I put on interviews served me well for many years as evidenced by the low turnover of staff and high productivity. There was one instance when we bent the rule and paid the price. There was a qualified biomedical scientist who had left the service to go and do various other jobs. She wanted to come back gradually to the service by 'shadowing' other people to regain experience and confidence. We agreed to this. She did this for a few months in the Canterbury laboratory. Then she made a request to move to the other laboratory at Margate. While there, an acute shortage of staff occurred – a few people unexpectedly left. Mr Fred Watson, a kind and wonderful gentleman, was the head of biomedical scientists and was based at Margate. He made a suggestion that the lady in question should be offered a permanent post; after all she had the qualifications. I did agree to his request – a decision I regretted as a catalogue of mistakes mounted. It was a difficult time. Luckily for us and for her, she acquired a spouse and they both went abroad. The lesson from this is that we did not go through the due process of a proper interview.

One of the features of the workforce we were proud of was the diversity of our staff. They came from different backgrounds. This helped the department in having different mind-sets and approaches when it came to solving problems. This was in contrast to some departments, which had a fairly homogenous work force.

Things progressed so fast that by year 2000 when I was interviewing for an infection control nurse, the human resources people were playing an increasing role in the process. Psychometric tests, which we eagerly embraced, were introduced. As more and more managers from outside the department got involved in the process of recruitment, we started getting unsuitable recruits with the expected decrease in retention of staff. This was not good for the department or for the new recruits as some left because of stress.

When the public health laboratory service took over the management of microbiology in East Kent, my role in the recruitment process diminished but I looked back in the earlier years when it was fun to welcome new blood in the department.

22

The Influence of a
Leader that Lasted for Ever

The Third January 1982 was the first day on the job as the consultant microbiologist in the Canterbury and Thanet Health District, which had two microbiology laboratories 18 miles apart – one at Canterbury and the other at Margate. I did not have a proper hand over as my single-handed predecessor Dr Ogilvie had retired a few months before. On the first day, I decided to get to know all the laboratory staff. The qualified technical staff were ranked as follows in ascending order of seniority: Medical Laboratory Scientific Officer 1 (MLSO 1), MLSO2, MLSO3 and MLSO4. The first person who came to my office at Canterbury was Charles Watson. He was an MLSO3 and head of the technical staff of Canterbury laboratory. He was a short man who walked with determined confidence. He seemed to know everybody in the area. He was a very useful source of information for me about the amenities in Canterbury. He started giving an account of who was who in the department. Then he said, 'I am really happy you've come'. As the conversation progressed, I discovered the reason for that statement. He and predecessor did not get on at all. After a few negative statements, I decided to meet all staff one by one. Mr Watson brought in the first one. She was Ann Pryce, an MLSO2 –very nice lady whose husband was a musician in the army. She later on proved to be a very reliable safe pair of hands. After a brief talk with her, she sent in the next person and so on until I had talked to all six. It was a small department.

In the afternoon, I went to Margate. There, I met Mr Fred Watson who was the MLSO4 and in charge of both laboratories. He spent most of his time at the Margate laboratory. The person who was in charge of day-to-day work at Margate was another wonderful and polite man called Graham Macklen. As at Canterbury, I talked to all staff one by one. In response to my question 'What is your interest?' a young trainee called Ricky said, 'Football. I am taking a month off to follow my team all over Europe'. I was rather surprised by his response as I was expecting him to say something connected with work. In fact after a month he went on his tour and never returned. This exercise of one to one talk with the staff paid dividends to my relationship with them. They could come to me and talk about anything concerning their work. I got to know their strengths and weaknesses. The talents I discovered in staff irrespective of rank included proofreading, organising events, photography to mention but a few. Eventually this process was largely replaced by formal appraisal.

I made the Canterbury laboratory my base spending most of the time there and only two afternoons (Wednesdays and Thursdays) at Margate.

There were rivalries and sometimes open hostilities between the staff at all levels of the two hospital. The staff in microbiology too had some differences of approach. We tried hard to standardise methods in the two laboratories but this effort was met with resistance. There was one incident, which was quite remarkable. The Margate laboratory had run out of a certain type of media (food for bacteria) and wanted to borrow some from Canterbury. On getting the request a senior person hid the media in the store where another person who was not aware of the plot found it days later.

I noticed that the staffs at Margate were very polite to each other, virtually copying what the head MLSO Fred Watson was doing. Without exception, they would include the words, 'Yes doctor' when they were addressing members of the medical staff including me – person who was working with them on daily basis. This continued even after Fred Watson had retired. Graham Macklen who was the second in command continued the tradition. This was testimony that head of a unit has a lot of influence on the behaviour on the people he/she leads. They will do good or bad things on his/her behalf to please the leader. That influence can linger on for years after the leader is gone.

There was a feeling of a family atmosphere. At around 11 am staff would gather in our small meetings/rest room for coffee break. Typically, I would drop in when everybody had settled down. This would usually be before or after my ward rounds. Placed in the middle of the coffee table would be a birthday cake decorated according to the interests of the person whose birthday was being celebrated. I remember a particular one in a form of a football pitch with goal posts and a ball! It was for a young trainee whose 'religion' was football. 'Doctor, would you like a piece of cake?' asked Carole our clerical officer.' A little piece,' I replied mindful of my weight problems at the time. Carole Thorpe was the person who made these beautiful birthday cakes. It seems she had a record of everybody's birthday. At these meeting, talking of football, there were two people who were keen fans of two football clubs – Arsenal and Manchester United. We really enjoyed teasing the person whose team had lost the previous day or weekend. We also had serious moments when we informally talked about work, current affairs. I would also talk about any microbiologically interesting case I had just seen on my ward rounds.

I enjoy watching relay races in athletics. I see similarities between a team of relay runners and successive leaders of an organisation or department. Hand overs and the performances of the individuals are crucial in both. Dropping a baton is catastrophic in relays and so is the selection of a dysfunctional leader for the long-term prospects of any organisation.

The way some modern organisations are run with the word 'reforms' in the air all the time affect employees in a different way. Everybody fights for survival. Some leaders use their units as stepping-stones to go to the top in record time. It should be remembered that it takes time for a good leader to have a lasting influence on an organisation.

About a year after my retirement, the small room was converted into an office. The whole laboratory was closed soon after but the good memories linger on. Occasionally, a few of us meet for a cup of coffee.

23

On Call Work that Made me Dog Tired

In 1982 when I started my job as consultant microbiologist in the Canterbury and Thanet Health District as it was then called, the on call (out of hours) service for microbiology was not satisfactory. When an urgent specimen was sent to the laboratory, the biomedical scientists in other departments like Clinical Biochemistry and Haematology processed the specimen. If they came across any problems, they would go through the list of senior staff in microbiology and call whoever was available to come in and help. On the Canterbury site before I arrived, the team of senior staff who volunteered to be on standby consisted of mainly two people – Dr Ogilvie, my predecessor and Dipti Sanyal. Dipti was a very remarkable young woman who did her work beyond the call of duty. She lived within walking distance of the hospital. She would come in even on Saturdays to do the work without pay.

My initial assessment led to the decision that a separate on call microbiology service had to be set up. With help of colleagues like Dr Ken Spittlehouse who was the consultant Chemical Pathologist and was also a member of the District Management Team, we managed to get funding for a robust on call microbiology service to cover the two main hospitals in the Health District.

The biomedical scientists were trained to inform the clinicians of urgent results (those that would lead to an immediate change in the management of the patient) by telephone. At the regular laboratory meetings, I would present and discuss interesting cases.

As time went on, we were all on the same 'wavelength' on what was to be done in different clinical scenarios. This was strengthened by detailed standard operation procedures (SOPs). Early morning, every Saturday, I went to the Canterbury laboratory and authorised all reports for inpatients so that they would be taken to the wards before the office staff went home at midday. A senior biomedical Scientist (BMS) would do the same at the Margate laboratory. For the rest of the weekend, I was contactable by telephone in cases of very serious infections or those that needed to be brought to the attention of the Public Health personnel. The latter included cases of meningitis and other infectious diseases, which were assessed to be highly contagious and as such would pose a major risk to the general public. My attitude towards the BMS was that they were highly professional people in whom I had a lot of trust. On top of that, we had very good SOPs, which they followed to the letter. Therefore, I was fully satisfied with the set-up we had.

I remember one Saturday morning, when as soon I walked into the Canterbury laboratory, one BMS brought to my attention an organism he had just identified as Listeria monocytogens, which can cause serious infections in people with weakened defences. This particular one was isolated from a middle-aged man who had presented with signs of meningitis. He had been started on the empirical therapy for meningitis but without much improvement. I straight away contacted Dr Ian Roberts, under whose care the patient was and we changed the therapy to Amoxicillin which was the drug of choice at the time for this organism. The following Monday, I found a large bottle of Champagne on my desk. On enquiring about this unexpected gift, I was informed that the patient had made a dramatic recovery after switching the antibiotics. Dr Roberts was gracious enough to tell the patient's wife that it was the laboratory staff who had contributed a lot to her husband's improved condition. She had rushed down to the local shop and bought this token of appreciation. A few months later, we put our gift to good use at the laboratory Christmas party.

We had sad stories as well, like that of a young woman who presented at around Christmas time with signs of severe meningococcal septicaemia. She too was under the care Dr Roberts who phoned at home to discuss her therapy. Despite our efforts, she did not make it. The following day, we isolated Neisseria meningitidis from her blood cultures – thus confirming the diagnosis. I went down to the post-mortem room to inform my histopathology colleagues of our findings. I had a quick glance at the body. She had a haemorrhagic rash all over. When I went back to the laboratory, I put the blood culture slide under the microscope to have another look at the tiny bacteria that had claimed the life the young woman.

For seventeen years, I managed the situation of being continuously on call except when I was on annual or study leave when consultant microbiologists from the neighbouring hospitals would cover for me. Most the time, Dr Graeme Calver consultant microbiologist at Maidstone covered for me and I returned the favour when he was away. He too had a good team headed by a very capable and efficient young man called Mark Holland. Therefore, there would be brief times when I would be on call for three hospitals as well as the community. There were moments when the workload was too much for one individual.

All that time I tried very hard to get a second consultant microbiologist with no success. The usual reason from managers was lack of funds. The other factor was that single-handed microbiologists were quite prevalent in the country at that time. Even if the funds were available, it would have been difficult to attract good candidates, as the laboratory at Margate was very small. In 1993, all that changed when we moved into a good well-furnished building at Margate. I redoubled my efforts to get a second microbiologist. Unfortunately around that time, people in Public Health Laboratory Service (PHLS) had other ideas. They wanted to provide the microbiology service including infection control for the whole of East Kent. Under their proposal, it was not necessary to appoint a microbiologist at Margate. As microbiology involved labour intensive work, my view was that the appointment should go ahead. On the back of accreditation for the laboratory at Margate, the senior managers at Thanet Healthcare Trust, as the hospital at Margate was called at the time, approved the appointment of a second consultant micro-biologist. We made the appointment but the person did not stay long for personal reasons.

The laboratories at Canterbury and Margate achieved full accreditation. In 1999, the Clinical Pathology Accreditation (CPA) inspectors made the following overview comment on the Canterbury laboratory:

'This is a well-equipped and well-organised department that provides a high quality service to the Hospital and local General Practitioners. The staff are well motivated and take a great deal of pride in their department. A repertoire of investigations is performed in the laboratory but it co-operates with other departments and nearby laboratories for the provision of some investigations. This enables it to ensure an efficient and rational service.

The interview with the users indicated good support from clinicians for both the analytical and clinical service provided by the laboratory. There is a high commitment to training, continuing education and professional development. There is a good internal education programme and evidence of attendance at external courses and conferences by all grades of staff. The documentation of methods and policies is very comprehensive and systems for keeping updated are in place and implemented. The workload is heavy for the number of staff in post, but it is probably sufficient for the current demand. However any increase in work would have adverse effect on the ability of medical laboratory and nursing staff to cope.'

This comment was the crowning experience of my career. I really felt that I had won my spurs. This was a moment to savour. It was very satisfying for me to have the CPA inspectors confirm that the staff had pride in their department and ownership of what they were doing. Building the true spirit of a laboratory or unit takes a long time. That is why I believe that unnecessary and frequent changes in departments are incompatible with this noble cause. The changes should be well thought through and organic. Those imposed from outside are unlikely to be successful in the long run.

It was a typical summer morning as I parked my car in the one of the five spaces that were allocated for consultant pathologists. There was one other car in the car park – a small Honda that belonged to Ann Pryce one of the senior biomedical scientist in Microbiology laboratory. I glanced at the laboratory – the lights were on but as I scanned all the windows I could not see anybody. I reached for my key but as I was about to insert it, the door swung open and out came one of the clinical chemistry biomedical scientist with his eyes half closed as he adjusted to the bright light outside. He politely held the door open for me. He looked tired. He must have been on call the whole night.

I headed for the open door of the microbiology laboratory. Standing in the doorway, I popped my head to see if Ann was sitting somewhere – there was nobody. I turned to walk to my office, I almost collided with her. She had just come out of the cold room carrying some reagents. 'Good morning Ann, you are nice and early today' I said as I gave way for her.

'Good morning, I dropped off my husband at the station. I thought I would make a head start as we are short of staff today,' she replied. She and others had done this sort of thing many times- putting in extra hours with no additional pay. I will be eternally grateful for the work they did.

This reminded me of a very capable young man called Steve Smith whose parents originally came from Jamaica. He was very keen to do research. He introduced a molecular technique called PCR (Polymerase chain reaction), which is now widely used in diagnostic laboratories. Unfortunately, before we could fully establish the technique in our laboratory, he moved to St Thomas's Hospital London, as plans to close the laboratory at Canterbury were confirmed.

In May 2001, the PHLS took over the running of the microbiology and infection control service for East Kent. The Canterbury microbiology laboratory was closed and the on call work was transferred to Ashford. The on call rota for consultant microbiologists had several people on it. The main advantage for me was that the days of being permanently on call were finally over. However, the workload and intensity of on call was huge.

The results of all urgent specimens were phoned by the on call consultant microbiologist. At night, the BMS would contact the microbiologist who would write down the results and phone the doctor on call who was usually the most junior member of the team. The weekend on call started on Friday at 5 pm. When it was my turn, I would rush home so that by that time the first call came, I would be ready with my pad and pen. The calls would come from the three hospitals – Ashford, Canterbury and Margate as well as General Practitioners. On Saturdays, I went to Ashford where I dealt with any queries and authorised reports. In the Ashford laboratory, I worked with very good and competent Biomedical Scientists. The senior staff included Marcus Coales, Rachael Arkley and Dr Mark Baker. The laboratory closed at 12 mid-day but I usually left at 1 o'clock.

I rushed home to wait for calls for the rest of the weekend, which ended at 9 am Monday morning. I would then brief my colleagues on the important cases of the weekend, only to start again at 5 pm. The on call period would end on Thursday morning at 9am. As we were four microbiologists, I did this approximately once a month. In a way this was better than being on call all the time, which I had done for seventeen years.

In the new era, several factors shaped the pattern and volume of the on call work for consultant microbiologists. The first factor was the relationship between the BMS (Biomedical Scientist) staff and the consultant microbiologists. The rationale for the BMS to give the urgent results to the microbiologist was that urgent treatment would be started by the microbiologist. Choice of the right treatment depends on many patient factors some of which the microbiologist may not be aware of, nor would the person receiving the results, who would in many instances be the most junior member of the clinical team. This practice increased the out of hours workload for consultant microbiologist without necessarily improving effective treatment. After all, there were good antimicrobial guidelines, which some clinicians did not use because they knew that the microbiologists were always available to give advice which sometimes was at variance with the guidelines leading to confusion.

The second interaction was between the microbiologist and the clinician in relation to infection control. Two pathogens were in the minds of the general public –Methicillin Resistant Staphylococcus aureus (MRSA) and Clostridium difficile (*see chapter 18*). This was whipped up by the media. As a result, the governments (of both main parties) set targets to reduce the rates of infections caused by the two pathogens. A lot of resources and effort were put in to meet the targets and I must say our hospitals did an excellent job. The key instruments used to do this job were a combination of taking strict infection control precautions and controlled antibiotic prescribing. For every infection that occurred a meeting of root cause analysis was held. Clinicians were put through their paces to explain the rationality of using a particular antibiotic. The main side effect of this practice was some clinicians became scared of getting it wrong. They left the responsibility of prescribing to their junior doctors who after all were getting many lectures on prescribing from the consultant microbiologists. Whenever there were doubts on how to manage an infection, they instructed their juniors to contact microbiologists. After a while, the training doctors started contacting consultant microbiologist without referring to their consultants. Telephoning consultant microbiologists day and night became the norm.

The correct diagnosis of an infection relies on taking detailed history, careful examination of the patient and ordering the right investigations. The most experienced clinician to do this would be the consultant clinician. The consultant microbiologists made themselves responsible to give advice on treatment based on information given by the most inexperienced member of the clinical team. I tried to persuade my colleagues to change this practice in vain. Each passing day, week and month, the situation got worse. I once received thirty calls on a Saturday.

About six months before I retired, the on call microbiologists had to take a laptop home and used it to gain secure access to the hospital computer systems. This created a platform where we worked as if we were at hospital but this time doing four peoples work. This involved looking for urgent results and phoning them; recording the calls and the advice given as well as authorising reports. The workload was intolerable. The mixture of sadness and frustration (knowing that things could be done better and with less pain) made me very exhausted. Any professional person should find his/her worker easier as time goes on. It is not a good situation when year thirty of your career is much worse than year one. Many people in similar situations will identify with this toxic combination of physical tiredness and frustration. When one meets difficult challenges like that, the temptation is to seek employment somewhere else. I had personal reasons not to do that. One of them was the excellent schools we had and still have in the area and the other was the risk of jumping from a frying pan into fire, as the core problems were institutional.

I look back with satisfaction in the knowledge that it was all done for patient care.

24

Embracing Change

All living things must adapt to change or suffer dire consequences. Changes in my life happened at different levels. As far as the job was concerned, there were those that occurred at national level in the form of major re-organisations and national guidelines and laws. There were also many that happened at hospital and departmental level. The changes should be for the benefit of patients as well as being fair to all health care staff involved. Changes should be implemented without compromising professional integrity.

'We are going to introduce a new test to detect...' were my typical opening words for an agenda item of the laboratory meeting of which I was the chairman. The laboratory meeting was the forum to introduce new tests. They were attended by all laboratory staff and held in the laboratory area so that all staff could attend. This resulted in more staff participating and savings on travel time. This also allowed all members of staff to have an input in the process and to become stakeholders. At these meetings I also presented interesting cases of the month to make sure all staff were closer to the patients whose specimen they were examining day in day out.

Senior members of staff went to many meetings including international ones to seek knowledge and new ways of doing things. If the new tests needed funding, business cases were promptly made. Allan Wilcox was the head biomedical scientist from 1985. He had one of the fastest response times to implement change. I would ask him to introduce a test and expect this to take days. To my pleasant surprise, all the paperwork would be on my desk the following day. He was instrumental in introducing computers to our two laboratories in the mid-1980s. He was helped by Geoff Mihr a Biomedical Scientist 3, who was based at the Canterbury laboratory. Geoff organised many educational meetings.

Changes also happened in antibiotic prescribing. Working with the Information Technology (IT) department in 1997, I formulated interactive antimicrobial guidelines. Unfortunately the key person in the IT department left and the project was abandoned, only to be revived more than ten years later. We had been emulating what was happening on the Internet.

One method I used to bring about change was at the time of interviewing the person I wanted to implement that change. In 2005, I wanted to introduce a system of estimating the antibiotic use so that I could compare the usage of antibiotics in different units of the hospital as well as detecting trends. The unit was the internationally recognised Defined Daily Dose (DDD) per patient – days. The antibiotic pharmacist we were about to recruit was going to be the person to monitor the usage. One of the questions, I asked her during the interview was about the unit. She got the job. Needless to state, the unit was successfully introduced in our hospitals.

One important aspect of change is legislation. As head of service, I made sure that I kept abreast of all the relevant legislation concerning health and safety as well as infection control and prevention. I remember going to the unit manager to get urgent funding for a health and safety issue. The manager was Dr Peggy Voysay. The equipment was ordered within minutes. This was the fastest course of action I had encountered so far. This was because there was no bureaucracy. It was also evidence of the trust Dr Voysay had in me. Professional people should be trusted but they too have to earn that trust.

Over the years, there were many reorganisations in our health district as well as at the national level. In many instances change was forced on us, but I made sure that change did not compromise my professionalism. The largest and most profound reorganisation at departmental level occurred in May 2001 when the Public Health Laboratory Service (PHLS) began to provide the microbiology and infection service for the whole of East Kent. This resulted in the closure of the laboratory at Canterbury and all staff becoming employees of the PHLS only to revert back to NHS employment in 2003. It is debatable if there were benefits to patient care, leave alone any financial benefits. How such changes affect the service users particularly patients is crucial. Centralisation should be done rationally: wholesale centralisation of a labour-intensive specialty like microbiology does not make sense. Answers to simple questions like these, can be revealing. Are more specimens lost? Are there more delays in getting results? Are results of a better quality? Do local young people have better chances of employment in the laboratory?

Some changes in the everyday work were dictated by the arrival of new pathogens. In March 2003, the spectre of SARS (Severe Acute Respiratory Syndrome) raised its ugly head. It was confirmed to be caused by a coronavirus. There was the expected panic because it was new. In subsequent years, others include the 'Bird Flu', which arrived in Europe in 2005. For all these, the laboratory had to adjust to cater for the new challenges. The changes also included eliciting a history of travel for patients who presented with community acquired respiratory infections and the type of isolation precautions we took when they were admitted.

It was Friday morning, 3 March 2004. I had just returned to my office after my ITU (Intensive Therapy Unit) round at Canterbury. I was quite happy the way it had gone that morning. Before I went to the ward round, I had looked up all the microbiology results and written them on a small piece of paper. The folded piece of paper had become my trademark to all the ITU staff. Whenever, I walked in, they expected me, to unfold it and give them results as we went around the unit discussing patients one by one. As I sat in my office, I realised that very little had changed from the days when I was a single-handed microbiologist. I was still looking after two ITUs – the one at Canterbury on Mondays and Fridays and the other three days at Margate. My three colleagues based at the main laboratory at Ashford looked after one ITU. This could not continue in perpetuity. I had not benefitted from the major change that had occurred in 2001. I had carried on for the sake of the patients in the two ITUs.

An idea came to me and that was to stay at Margate all the time and develop another functional unit – Microbiology – Respiratory Medicine. I was getting on very well with chest physicians at Margate. These are physicians who specialise in the management of respiratory diseases including asthma and tuberculosis. Turning, the laboratory at Margate into 'respiratory laboratory' I thought would be a wonderful idea, after all, the laboratory already had some good equipment for investigating tuberculosis. In addition to that, the laboratory would perform rapid tests using molecular technology to detect other respiratory pathogens like Mycoplasma pneumoniae, Chlamydophila pneumoniae and the Flu viruses to mention but a few. All these pathogens cause pneumonia. This would enable clinicians to make more accurate diagnosis soon after patients were admitted or send those who were not very ill home with a diagnosis. This would also lead to the use of fewer antibiotics. At the time, patients with community-acquired pneumonia were put on combinations of antibiotics to cover all possible causative organisms. If the laboratory was able to detect the causative pathogen within hours of admission, antibiotics would be used to target that pathogen saving a lot of money in the process and reducing the risk of resident organisms becoming resistant. This was a dream plan.

Fast forward to 20 April 2004. When this plan was presented to a meeting of senior managers in pathology, it was flatly rejected. I felt deflated and dejected. The major announcements at that meeting were the approval of the appointment of a biomedical scientist 3 who would be the quality manager and the planned transfer of GP work from Margate to Ashford. I continued to cover the two ITUs for another six years. The laboratory at Margate was slowly downgraded and eventually closed in 2013 – a year after my retirement. This was a unidirectional change. I believe that change that takes into account good ideas from all participants is likely to have long lasting benefits to an organisation.

Rapid change may be inevitable but it should be well thought through and balanced with stability, which is necessary for the proper evaluation of the change and wellbeing of the people affected.

The other changes were social. These are equally important as they are bound to affect ones work in a positive and negative way. The first one was the change in my marital status when my first wife, Rebecca and I were divorced in 1987 after 13 years of marriage. I should point out that neither of us blamed the other for this sad event. The period following that was quite a challenge. Apart from my close family, I had good friends to help me. They included Sarah and Sam Zimbe, a wonderful couple, who frequently invited me to their home. Ten years later, in 1996, I married my current wife Lillian and together we have a wonderful son called Suubi.

The other changes were the loss of my parents, my father in 1996 at the age of ninety and my mother in 2003 at the age of ninety-two. I missed their immense love and kindness. They taught me the concepts of sense of duty and hard work, which proved invaluable. Their job entailed moving to different parts of Uganda and adapting to new dialects and customs. All this primed me to embrace change in my own life.

The political changes in Uganda affected me and my family. There were wars and coups over many years. In the summer of 1986, I went back to Uganda for an emotional visit. I had been away for eleven years. The country was recovering from years of wars. Inflation was very high. People had to carry sacks of money around. It was nice to see people I had not seen for a long time.

Another wonderful and joyous moment in my life was the birth of my first grandson, Harry in 2013. He was born to Bobby and Tracey Ndawula who gave us a wonderful wedding in 2010.

25

My Oasis of Peace and Tranquility

It was a very hot Friday afternoon. My watch read 4.30pm. It was time for my weekly visits to the Chaucer Hospital – a private hospital about half a mile from the Kent and Canterbury Hospital. My car was like an oven – so by the time I arrived I was hot and sweating. It was a wonderful feeling when I opened the door and stepped in the laboratory, which was air-conditioned. The feeling was only matched by the happy and smiling faces of all the staff. This was the Friday routine for more than 20 years.

I first worked at the Chaucer in 1983 when the hospital had just opened. At the time, consultant pathologists who were working in the NHS health district formed a partnership we called Kent Pathology Services (KPS). The members included Dr Harold Sterndale (Haematologist), Dr Yvonne Williams (Haematologist), Dr George Gibson (Histopathologist), Dr Malcolm Farley (Histopathologist), Dr Ken Spittlehouse (Chemical Pathologist) and me (Microbiologist).

A few years later the group was joined by Dr Paul Buamah (Chemical Pathologist) and Dr Mark Winter (Haematologist). The partnership worked very well. We took turns to represent KPS on the Medical Advisory Committee of the hospital. Each member of the group used their unique expertise to help others, for example Dr Sterndale advised the group on financial matters and was responsible for distributing the fees. I always looked forward to the time he would give me a call or entered my office and say 'Emmanuel, I have got some money for you'. Others like Dr Gibson did a lot of work on contract negotiations for KPS.

As time passed, it became very clear that the work pattern and contribution to the 'money pot' from each varied according to the pathology speciality. Consequently after a while, KPS was disbanded and instead each speciality had a separate contract with the hospital.

As a microbiologist I found the biomedical scientists a dream team to work with. They were highly professional and polite to all people who used the laboratory. For a long time, the team was under the able leadership of Terry Hobson one of the nicest people I had the pleasure of knowing.

Infection control was another area I enjoyed. As all patients were in single rooms, cross infection rarely happened. The infection control meetings were brief and to the point. This is because, all the people who attended the meeting were busy and they always had something they were rushing to after the meeting.

In later years, we had one annual meeting with the Executive Director. At the meeting, we reviewed the activities of the previous year. The unique thing about these was that the Executive Director was just an observer – letting the professional people do their job. The other good feature of these meeting was that all pathologists were invited. They were all stakeholders. Unlike in the NHS, a histopathologist could not represent a microbiologist, nor would a haematologist represent a chemical pathologist. They all do different things. A chemical pathologist should not be expected to give the right answer to unexpected question concerning microbiology.

On the NHS side, over the years, discussions on the mergers of laboratories took place. The proponents of mergers always used the argument that small laboratories would not survive. My argument was always that it was not the size of the laboratory but the quality and the professionalism of the workers in the laboratory that mattered. I used to give the Chaucer as an example of a small laboratory that remained small and efficient. During the time I worked at the Chaucer, I learned that outside organisations had made attempts to provide the laboratory services to the hospital and had failed to do so.

Unlike the NHS hospitals where I mainly dealt with junior doctors, at the Chaucer, consultants contacted and gave me detailed and accurate information about their patients. Consequently, I would give more accurate advice. As time went on, most senior consultants would contact me less and less as they learnt to deal with most infection scenarios. They also learnt to use the antimicrobial guidelines, which I had formulated for them. For many years, the income I received from the Chaucer was very modest. In any case, I had to abide by the '10% NHS rule of reducing the NHS salary if one did significant amount of private work. In the final year of employment, I re-negotiated my contract for a better pay. Looking back, it was a good strategy not to price myself out of a fulfilling job. When I retired from my NHS job, I also gave up my work at the Chaucer. A newly appointed and good microbiologist Dr Srinivasulu Reddy succeeded me.

All in all, this was indeed an oasis of peace and tranquillity for me but suffice to state that the quality of service I gave both organisations was identical.

26

At Last I Retire

My alarm clock went off as it had done many mornings before at 6.00am. I stretched and switched it off. I turned to my wife Lillian and said in Luganda 'Wasuze otya' meaning 'Good morning'. This was no ordinary morning. It was 30 March 2012. My last day to work as a consultant microbiologist. I went through the routine-bathroom, dress up, light breakfast, picked my twenty-year-old green briefcase and rushed to the car. As I approached the car, I knew that later in the day when I parked it in the same spot I would have retired. At the end of my journey at the other end, the hospital car park was relatively empty – one of the reasons why I always went in early and the other being light traffic at that time in the morning. I used a key to go through the side door, which was very near my office. As I entered the office, I noticed that it was very empty. I had removed most all my books, journals and other personal possessions. As soon as I sat down, there was a knock at the door. It was the cleaner. Cleaners were the first people I talked to in the morning.

'It is my last day – I am retiring', I told him.

'Oh, but you look very young doctor,' he responded looking surprised.

'Ah—don't be fooled by the appearances', I replied feeling a bit flattered.

More laboratory staff arrived. There was only one topic for discussion – the last day. I reminded them of the farewell do – time and venue. It was time to do my last ward round. In the last few years, I had been accompanied by Claire Manning who was the antimicrobial pharmacist at Margate, but she was currently a way on maternity leave. So, I went on my own to Intensive Care Unit, which I had visited for years. It was the only unit where I always discussed patients with consultants. I talked to them about the guidelines on antibiotics and infection control issues, which passed on to their staff. It was an example of good functional multi-disciplinary team. They were like family to me. Therefore, this being the last day I was quite emotional.

Next, I went to the admissions ward where I found a group of doctors discussing a patient with pneumonia. As soon as they saw me, they said in a 'business as usual tone', 'Dr Ndawula, can you please advise us of the most suitable antibiotic for this patient who is allergic to many antimicrobial drugs?'

After giving the advice, I said to the young doctors, 'this is the last patient I am going to deal with. I am retiring today and I am going to my farewell party right now'.

The party was in a small room, which the pathology secretary managed to get, as there was a scramble for rooms at lunchtime. Professor Fritz Muhlschlegel, head service at the time, Dr James Nash, Director of Infection prevention and Control and Dr Ken Adegoke, consultant intensivist spoke. They were very generous in thanking me for my contributions to the organisation.

'This is one of the happiest moments of my entire working life. I have come to the end of a long journey, which has been full of ups and downs. Today, I am going to concentrate on the ups', were my opening remarks in response. I went on to thank the various groups I had worked with over a period of thirty years in East Kent. I also thanked them for the wonderful gifts and cards one of which was really huge –containing interesting messages from various people.

I went back to the laboratory to collect my green briefcase. I said my last farewells to the microbiology staff some of whom I worked with for decades. They included Dave Chetywnd, Dave Bissessur, Helen Smith and Roberta Bourlett. Then I turned to Richard and said, 'Let's do this'. Richard Edwards was a young and very polite trainee biomedical scientist who had on many occasions helped to lock the door behind me so that I did not have to fumble to get keys to lock the door. It had been a long-standing joke that one day he would lock the door behind me for the last time.

'With pleasure, I will lock the door', he said with a big beaming smile.

At around 2.30 on a sunny Friday afternoon, I got into my car and drove away. In the rear mirror, I could see the door to the laboratory disappearing in a distance. Little did I know at the time that the laboratory would close the following year (2013).

A few days later it really sank in that I was really free from what I often referred to as 'THEY' or 'THEM'. They, who influence what you say, write, wear to mention but a few. It was liberating to be free of all that.

I continue to ponder and reflect. I get very excited when I get an idea or take a course of action, which makes me a better person.

27

My Interest in Music

I was eleven years old. It was about nine o'clock Saturday night. We had just finished our dinner of matooke (mashed plantain) and groundnut source. My father started singing one of the familiar hymns, signalling that it was time for evening prayer. We all joined in as we gathered in the sitting room. My father sat at the table with a paraffin lantern nearby, giving just adequate light for him to read a passage from the Bible. We were now on the second verse; my mother was sitting just behind me. I could hear very clearly her beautiful soft voice almost yodelling in some parts. I decided to sing the third verse in alto. My father would then put extra words, which would be adlibs of modern music. It sounded great.

The following day, Sunday, my father and I would go to the 'kigango', which was some sort of shade where the church drums were kept. We would bring them out and start sounding the first of the three sessions of drums before the church service at ten o'clock. I got the sense of rhythm from these wonderful instruments. During the morning services, I enjoyed singing hymns. A great friend of mine at the time was a boy called Gordon Bukenya. Gordon had the opposite of a perfect pitch. That did not deter him singing as loudly as his lungs could allow. Sitting near him was quite a challenge to say the least.

My other source of music was the radio. We bought our first radio in the late 1950s. It was a 'PYE model – PE 37 – c1951', which had a huge battery and an aerial which was placed on the top of a long pole outside the house, so neighbours would know which house had just bought a radio! To preserve the battery, my father insisted on our radio being used for only the news and announcements, especially the obituaries. My sisters, my brother and I were more interested in listening to music. Our favourite programme was one in which listeners sent messages and a popular song of their choice to their loved ones. The only chance we had to listen to these songs was when our father was away on parish visits and mother busy working in the garden. Other times, we would hide behind the bushes near our neighbour's house and listen to his very loud radio. God bless him.

When I moved to Kako Junior School in 1960, I joined the school choir, which had the privilege of sitting very near the altar opposite and facing the girls' choir. You can imagine the secret glances that went on between the two choirs. Joking apart, the sounds of the melodies were just amazing.

In the school main hall, there was an old piano. It was my first sight of a piano. I was attracted to it like a bee to a flower. During lunchtime, I watched a boy called Kohl Lubega playing popular folk songs as well as songs that were popular on the radio. As soon as he left, I would sit down and imitate what he had been playing. Eventually, I mastered a few chords that enabled me to play my own tunes. I was hooked. I looked for any opportunity the piano was not in use to play a new tune.

In 1962, I went to Kings College Budo. This was a very good school, which was a paradise for music development. I joined the chapel choir as well the prestigious choir called the Nightingales. The latter was interesting because we sang all types songs including many English folk songs, Negro spirituals to mention but a few. Later on I started having piano lessons but the temperament of the piano teacher forced me to give it up. I however continued playing by ear. What I was really interested in was creative music. I also developed an interest in playing the guitar. I had brief practices on many guitars owned by boys in the school. I would hang around the owner's bed and ask him for chance to play but occasionally I would 'borrow' the instrument in his absence.

One of the most memorable musical events was in 1966 when inter house singing competitions were held. Each house had to sing two songs – one in English and the second had to be a traditional African song. As I was the only person in my house that belonged to any choir, I volunteered to lead my house. I had to select people who had ability and interest to sing. I chose an assistant to lead in the African song. The coaching took place at weekends and in the evenings just before bedtime. We came second to one of the girl's houses. The consolation was that all the members of the winning team were in choirs. I felt good and proud of that achievement.

In a vacation of 1965, I went to Nairobi Kenya to take part in a USA sponsored 'Moral Re-Armament' conference. At very short notice (48 hours), we formed a small musical group and wrote a song, which we performed to the delegates. The lyrics of the song were in line with the theme of the conference. Going by the applause we got, I think the audience enjoyed our performance. This was the beginning of my creative work.

I suspended my music activities when I went to medical school and long after that when I was a busy doctor.

Fast forward while in the UK in early 1992, I revived my interest in music when I bought my first keyboard. As I played, I created melodies and then lyrics. I had a 'do it yourself' attitude at the time, so I bought some recording equipment and started recording all tunes that came to my head.

Like father, my son Jonathan Ndawula had tremendous interest in music. His idol was Michael Jackson. He would dress, sing and dance like him. He also had a very creative mind. He started writing and performing his own songs. I bought an ADAT recording system and recorded many of our songs. Jonathan did a number of gigs at various events organised by the Ugandan community in London. Some time ago when the King of Buganda – Muwenda Mutebi II came to London, he met young people who sang, 'Ekitiibwa Kya Buganda' (the national anthem of the Kingdom). Jonathan played the accompaniment on piano. He felt really proud to have done that in the presence of the King.

My philosophical mind had very strong views on various issues. I decided to express these in the lyrics of my songs. '*I'm Happy*' was one the first songs I wrote in 1994. I have always been interested in the deeper meaning of words or phenomenon with a view of helping me to be a better person. I decided to lower my threshold for happiness to just being alive and not to make happiness conditional to anything else. Anything above that level, I regarded as 'happier'. Then I went on to mention a few scenarios. Closely related to this issue was a song called, *'You've Got To Be Positive'*. Over years, this has the really lifted my spirits when I was feeling low. Another favourite of my mine, which I wrote in the same year was, *'Thank You'* in which I listed gifts I had received over the years. The one I valued most was love. That is why I say, **'Love is the mother of all gifts'**. On the other side the coin, 'Lack of it is the source of many unpleasant things'.

One of the greatest surprises, I have ever had was when, Paulo Ndawula, my youngest son at the time said to me, 'Dad, will you please look at the songs I have written?' He opened his folder. My jaw dropped. There were more than thirty songs in that folder. 'When did you start doing this?' I asked in disbelief. 'A few years ago', he said casually. He was 15 when he revealed his secret. He started singing the first song he wrote. It was called, *'Teach Me How To Love'*

I could not believe the quality of his voice and the maturity of his lyrics. I put my stuff on hold and started recording his stuff. In 1999, he participated in a children's BBC World Service programme in which some of his songs were played. We later decided to put his music on hold while he pursued his studies.

I continued with mine but as I had a very busy job, I had to do music during holidays and weekends. Many friends always asked me how I managed to find time to do music in my life as a doctor. My answer was always the same, 'If you have a passion for something, you will find time to do it'. I was one of many professional people who have interests in other fields. After my retirement I am enjoying it even more as I have a lot more time to explore many aspects of this wonderful pastime of mine.

The experience of writing a song, recording it and listening to the finished product is one of the most wonderful things that can happen to a singer/song writer. At the beginning of March, under the Group name 'Optimum Music' we released two albums to all major music digital outlets. The two were: '*I'm Happy*' by me – Emmanuel Ndawula and '*Always*' by Jonathan Ndawula. This was soon followed by '*Shine*' by Paulo Ndawula. Our performances so far have been mainly done through music videos which we love producing.

When I reflect on what music means to me, I go back to basics. I put human needs into two categories-basic and desirable. The basic needs include food, air and shelter (the latter includes protection from any harm) among others. There are people who use music to earn a living – essentially putting food on the table. The desirable needs improve our wellbeing which include pleasure and love – thus, 'If music be the food of love, play on...' in Shakespeare's *Twelfth Night*. So far I have used music to communicate all sorts of emotions and ideas. This has been very fulfilling.

28

Reflections

Like many other people, I have had many instances in my life when I paused, thought hard and realised what was important. Sometimes, the ideas and resolutions were triggered by a misfortune. I usually jotted them down in my dairies or included them in a song I would be writing at the time. In this chapter, it is gratifying to share them with other people. Here is a mixed bag of them:

'Life is too short to be worrying all the time'. This was a line I included in a song I wrote in 1994 called *'Let us celebrate'*, which always spiced many celebrations I had over the years. The celebrations included birthdays, anniversaries and family achievements. I would say to myself and to those around me 'Let's enjoy this NOW'. It is a concept of living life to full.

In 1995, I wrote a song entitled *'Your Market Value'*. It proposes a notion that everybody has a market value in society and that the value depends on one's activities, behaviour, personality, talent, work ethics among others I listed these in the lyrics. On one extreme, a person who is one in a million will have a very high market value. I strive to increase my market value and try to avoid those activities that devalue me. I often shared this notion with my children and friends.

The following year, 1996, I wrote another song entitled, *'Have I Done Enough To Be Trusted?'* It was supposed to be a response to a question, 'Don't you trust me?' or to a plea, 'Please, trusts me'. In the song I suggest that the onus should be on the person who wants to be trusted to prove their trustworthiness, which depends on his/her previous activities and what they are currently doing.

In 1997, I wrote a song called, '*He Said*' which I dedicated to my father who had passed away on 1996. It was based on some of the things he used to tell me as a code of conduct for a successful and meaningful life. Three lines in the lyrics stand out for me. The first one is 'Never forget where you come from. It is the core of who you are'. I hope that this resonates with many people. The second one is 'Do to others as you want them to do to you'. On reflection, I have added another dimension to the obvious interpretation and that is other people's priorities may not be the same as mine. I should be conversant with the list of things they love and things they are not fond of. The third line in the song was 'Never take revenge because in the end you will be the loser'. This is quite difficult to achieve because in many cases provocation can be unbearable.

The other song worth mentioning is called '*I'm Really Sorry*' which I wrote in 1997. One of the main reasons for conflicts and unhappiness to continue festering is the absence of proper closure. One way of achieving this is for injured party to receive a proper apology. The lyrics of the song exhibit what I think is a proper apology.

For years, one of the most intriguing issues for me was 'happiness' and indeed it has been a topic for many discussions and debates. In 2012, I revised the song entitled '*I'm Happy*' which I first wrote in the early 1990s (see *chapter 27*). My take on it was to regard being alive and reasonably healthy as the lowest denominator of happiness. Anything above that is a bonus and should make one happier. That was the concept of the song in which I listed several things that made me happier and they included group happiness, love, kindness, beauty and reward for hard work.

On 8 July 2013, I wrote this down in my diary; 'the choices we make every second, minute, hour, day, week, month and year determine who we are. It is vital that we avail ourselves of as many opportunities as possible so that we have many choices to select from.' This has deep and relevant meaning to me. As we all know, what people chose to do has consequences that affect them as well as other people. Whenever,

I make mistakes, I learn from them but not spend a lot of time regretting.

On 9 November 2013, I made a resolution that I had to become a better and happier person by making some rules to control my mind set. Over the years, I had observed that the words or phrases people frequently used were reflections of their mind-sets. Those with problematic mind-sets often used words or phrases like "It is sad –" I miss…'I hate…' 'Let us send a clear message to so and so that we are…'

The general rule I made for myself was as follows: 'If it is likely to cause anger, irritation, embarrassment, hatred, misery, then DON'T SAY OR DO IT'.

The good mind set words/phrases include 'I love…', 'I have got enough provisions…' and 'Let me share with you' (rather than giving unsolicited advice).

I made a resolution to use more of such good words/phrases. The general rule I made for myself was: 'Only do it if it is likely to cause happiness, pleasure, and prosperity to you and to other people (without breaking the law).'

It is not easy to keep to these rules but I am trying my best. I was once having conversation with a close friend of mine. The topic was 'unconditional love'. We talked about couples we both knew – some very happy and others not so happy. He was of the opinion that one should give unconditional love to certain groups of people including their children and spouses. My view was that the love you give a person should not be affected by things that person cannot change or are beyond control, for example appearance, illness and such like. To these unconditional love applies. It should not apply to activities of clear choice like being unfaithful, breaking the law and disobedience in case of children. My friend shook his head in disagreement. He started talking about the chemistry of the brain and hormones affecting peoples' behaviour inferring some people could not control their actions and therefore unconditional love applies to them too. I stood up, shook his hand and said, 'We have agreed to disagree on this matter'.

I was once talking to a young man called Steve Smith about my experiences in East Kent. Steve was a bright Biomedical

Scientist whose parents came from Jamaica. He wondered how I had managed to survive in my post for so long. Like a flash I told him, 'hard work and keeping ones nose clean'. I went on to say that it had not been easy especially as a person of colour. As a passionate believer of the concept of hard work and reward, I had been disappointed many times. I remember one February afternoon in 2001 reading yet another letter of regret for not having been given a merit award. It was signed by the regional manager of the Public Health Laboratory Service (PHLS), which had just taken over the provision of the microbiology service of East Kent. In my heart of hearts, I knew that I deserved an award for the hard work I had done the previous year against the background of the major reorganizational changes that had taken place. The appeal process revealed that some of the references and citations provided for my application left a lot to be desired. After the initial shock, I got over it and continued with my work. Such instances test our ability to stick to our core principles and values.

One of my favourite proverbs is 'Birds of a feather, flock together'. Of late I have seen its applications in many spheres of life. Take business for example: a good business team is necessary for success. The team members will have different skills but should have the same key goals for that particular business. Many people including myself have learnt that the hard way, the pitfall being to recruit team members on basis of being family members, friends, and countrymen among others.

On the 5 December 2013, when President Nelson Mandela passed way, I sent a text to my son Bobby, 'We are lucky to have lived in the same period as this great man'. This is an opportunity for me to write something about this great and inspirational leader. He taught us forgiveness among many other values. He also showed us true leadership. As a leader, doing what is popular is the easy option. The test for true leadership is to do what may be unpopular at the time but is the right course of action for the long-term benefit of the people.

As mentioned in the last chapter, in 1965, I attended a 'Moral Re-Armament' conference in Nairobi. At that conference we sang a song part, of which lyrics went something like this, 'you can't live crooked and think straight: whether you are a worker or chief of state. So build your nation before it is too late. But you can't live crooked and think straight.' That is all I will write on the very important topic of corruption, which affects, to varying degrees, all nations and organisations all over the world.

After retirement, I have had more time to reflect on many issues. Resetting my mind-set has helped me to reassess my values and priorities. I have realised that the level of importance I attach to anything is my choice. I continue to reflect on life and hopefully becoming a wiser and a better person.

When I look at the beautiful satellite images of mother earth, I get a strong feeling that mankind and all other living organisms should be closer as we all inhabit the same planet.

Index